EMPOWERING
YOUTH

How to Encourage Young Leaders to Do Great Things

KELLY CURTIS, M.S.

Empowering Youth: How to Encourage Young Leaders to Do Great Things
Kelly Curtis, M.S.

The following are registered trademarks of Search Institute: Search Institute®, Developmental Assets®, and

Search Institute Press
Copyright © 2008 by Search Institute

All rights reserved. No parts of this publication may be reproduced in any manner, mechanical or electronic, without prior permission from the publisher except in brief quotations or summaries in articles or reviews, or as individual activity sheets for educational use only. For additional permission, write to Permissions at Search Institute.

At the time of publication, all facts and figures cited herein are the most current available; all telephone numbers, addresses, and Web site URLs are accurate and active; all publications, organizations, Web sites, and other resources exist as described in this book; and all efforts have been made to verify them. The author and Search Institute make no warranty or guarantee concerning the information and materials given out by organizations or content found at Web sites that are cited herein, and we are not responsible for any changes that occur after this book's publication. If you find an error or believe that a resource listed herein is not as described, please contact Client Services at Search Institute.

10 9 8 7 6 5 4 3
Printed on acid-free paper in the United States of America.

Search Institute
615 First Avenue Northeast, Suite 125
Minneapolis, MN 55413
www.search-institute.org
612-376-8955 • 800-888-7828

ISBN-13: 978-1-57482-254-0

Library of Congress Cataloging-in-Publication Data
Curtis, Kelly, 1969-
    Empowering youth : how to encourage young leaders to do great things / by Kelly Curtis.
        p. cm.
    Includes bibliographical references and index.
    ISBN-13: 978-1-57482-254-0 (pbk. : alk. paper)
    ISBN-10: 1-57482-254-3 (pbk. : alk. paper)
    1. Youth development. 2. Community leadership.
    3. Social work with youth. I. Title.
HQ796.C97 2008
362.7083—dc22
                                    2008003110

Credits
Editor: Susan Wootten
Book Design: Percolator
Production Supervisor: Mary Ellen Buscher

About Search Institute Press
Search Institute Press is a division of Search Institute, a nonprofit organization that offers leadership, knowledge, and resources to promote positive youth development. Our mission at Search Institute Press is to provide practical and hope-filled resources to help create a world in which all young people thrive. Our products are embedded in research, and the 40 Developmental Assets—qualities, experiences, and relationships youth need to succeed—are a central focus of our resources. Our logo, the SIP flower, is a symbol of the thriving and healthy growth young people experience when they have an abundance of assets in their lives.

Licensing and Copyright
The checklists in *Empowering Youth: How to Encourage Young Leaders to Do Great Things* may be copied as needed. For each copy, please respect the following guidelines: Do not remove, alter, or obscure the Search Institute credit and copyright information on any handout. Clearly differentiate any material you add for local distribution from material prepared by Search Institute. Do not alter the Search Institute material in content or meaning. Do not resell handouts for profit. Include the following attribution when you use the information from the handouts in other formats for promotional or educational purposes: **Reprinted with permission from *Empowering Youth: How to Encourage Young Leaders to Do Great Things*, by Kelly Curtis, M.S. (specify the title of the handout). Copyright © 2008 by Search Institute Press, Minneapolis, Minnesota, 800-888-7828, www.search-institute.org. All rights reserved.**

Printing Tips
To produce high-quality, inexpensive copies of handouts for distribution, follow these tips: Always copy from the original. Copying from a copy lowers the reproduction quality. Make copies more appealing by using brightly colored paper or colored ink. Quick-print shops often run daily specials on certain colors of ink. For variety, print each handout on a different color of paper. Make two-sided copies if printing more than one handout or a multipage handout. Ensure the weight of the paper is heavy enough (at least 60-pound offset paper) to prevent text from becoming visible on the opposite side, as often happens with 20-pound paper.

Contents

Acknowledgments

Even well into the second hour of my 55th interview for this book, I felt no desire to end the conversation. On the phone far longer than planned, I continued to be riveted by the words of yet another asset builder, one of dozens from around the globe. And I felt *energized*. You can't talk to people like these leaders and not feel good. If it weren't for looming deadlines and *life*, I'd still be chatting—headphone hooked to my ear, racking up free long-distance minutes.

Dozens of interviews became one long chain of asset champions—each referring to five more individuals who had impacted a community in tremendous ways. I feel privileged to have had the opportunity to connect with this asset-rich group of colleagues. It's been an inspiring journey.

As you read, you'll find firsthand accounts and stories from asset champions around the world. Some of their names are easily recognizable in the asset arena, while others are less well known, but they have all made a similarly dynamic impact on their communities. My sincere thanks to all of you who are named in these chapters—adults who lent their significant expertise, as well as youth who provided their valuable perspective.

This book would still be just an enthusiastic e-mail if my colleague, Kathleen Kimball-Baker, hadn't given the idea such a fine endorsement. And I couldn't have asked for a warmer, more professional introduction to the complicated world of publishing than the one I received from Search Institute's former director of publishing, Claudia Hoffacker, who skillfully ushered my proposal through editorial channels. I'll never know all the Search Institute professionals who left their mark on this book—in publishing, editing, marketing, and research—as well as the internal and external reviewers who offered thoughtful comments on the preliminary manuscript. The questions and concerns they shared ultimately strengthened the content.

The one individual I've depended upon more than anyone during this project is my capable editor, Susan Wootten. Her insightful questions and careful revisions have coached and encouraged me as I put words to the page. Her expert use of language is found in nearly every paragraph of this book.

Thanks to Marilyn Peplau—my longtime mentor in the asset approach—for her wealth of connections throughout the global asset community, and for being the first to demonstrate for me *how* to empower young people.

And of course, I hold a special place in my grateful heart for my personal empowerment team—Wayne, Deena, Curtis, and Mom. Thank you for the support and inspiration you provided during those long months at the keyboard . . . and always.

Introduction

"This was the first time I had been part of the creation of something, rather than just the execution. I had thought my role in this organization would be as a worker for adults, not as an innovator supported by adults. This experience had a profound impact on me as a watershed moment where I was given responsibility and power in a very real project."

—DANIEL GILLESPIE, 20, YALE UNIVERSITY STUDENT AND FORMER MEMBER
OF THE ALASKA SPIRIT OF YOUTH ORGANIZATION

Empowerment—a decade ago, this buzzword wouldn't have meant much to me. But within a month of starting my position as school counselor at New Richmond High School in Wisconsin, I *knew* what it meant: Something was different here. The school was unlike any place I'd ever been. And then, like the resolution that occurs after staring at a three-dimensional design until the hidden picture emerges, it became clear to me what that difference was—youth had a *voice*.

You could hear it. See it. Feel it. Excitement was palpable in the halls, on the walls, in the library and offices. At every turn, young people played an important role in the life of their school. An eleventh-grade student answered the office telephone. Tenth graders designed and painted a dramatic mural. A twelfth grader brainstormed ideas with the principal, preparing to make an important presentation to the school board. Youth-designed posters hung on many of the walls. Students were entrusted with the use of expensive computer equipment from the technology room.

In this environment, youth ideas thrived and genuine motivation reigned. Youth took leadership in school decision making and activities. They voiced their opinions freely and offered their ideas regularly. This atmosphere of empowerment had been carefully cultivated for years before I arrived. The climate was unique. Youth were regarded as assets in their school—people whose talents were utilized and whose voices were heard.

Youth empowerment in all its forms is a *process*, with doable, defined steps leading toward it. While some ideas, tips, and activities in this book may seem initially beyond your reach or may not fit your current programming, understand that the empowerment process allows for gradual integration of new practices into existing structures. And because positive adult attitudes are critical to youth empowerment, creating an environment that's receptive enough to foster youth empowerment can sometimes take awhile.

Organizations with a strong base of adults who know how to help youth find their voice are better prepared to pursue projects that rely heavily on an empowerment mind-set. Empowering attitudes and beliefs must exist in order to sustain and support youth programming. Behind the various strategies outlined here is a philosophy that matters. As is true with asset building, empowerment isn't a program—it's a way of thinking. Pat Howell-Blackmore, director of communications and programs for Thrive! The Canadian Centre for Positive Youth Development, explains:

> A place that is rich in Empowerment assets shows evidence that empowerment is present from the moment you walk in the door. If it's a school or youth center, does a [young person] greet you? Are youth [assuming] leadership . . . roles in the activities that are taking place? Are youth engaged in tasks that have a direct impact on other youth? You don't necessarily hear adult voices—but you will see smiling adult faces, happy to help, support, and encourage. You see adults who are not afraid to defer to a young person to provide a service, support, or direction. You see young people and adults who are comfortable with their interactions and roles in the community.

At Search Institute, a Minnesota-based youth development research organization, we speak of 40 Developmental Assets—the qualities, opportunities, and conditions that characterize the lives of healthy, happy, and resilient young people. The Developmental Assets are distributed across eight general categories: Support, Empowerment, Boundaries and Expectations, Constructive Use of Time, Commitment to Learning, Positive Values, Social Competencies, and Positive Identity. Ongoing studies consistently show that the more Developmental Assets young people have in their lives, the more likely it is that they'll avoid risky behaviors and thrive developmentally.

Search Institute identifies six guiding principles to help communities think through the process of building Developmental Assets in youth:

- All young people need assets.
- Everyone can build assets.
- Asset building is an ongoing process.
- Healthy relationships—between adults and young people, and young people and their peers—are key.
- Asset builders send consistent messages of support to the young people in their lives.
- Repetition of positive messages in one area strengthens and reinforces asset building in other areas.

For a complete list of the 40 Developmental Assets, see page 139.

About This Book

This book focuses on the development of the Empowerment assets in young people: the ways in which a community lets young people know they are valued, treats young people as important resources, provides the opportunities and means for youth to genuinely serve others, and helps young people feel safe enough to grow into confident leaders. You may not realize it or may think it's beyond your reach, but if you come into contact with children and teenagers in *any* capacity, you have opportunities every day to empower them.

You'll find straightforward descriptions of the Empowerment assets, stories from caring adults in action, self-assessment checklists for youth-serving organizations and communities, and hands-on strategies to encourage asset development in young people. You'll also find tips, activities, and help from asset leaders all over the world who share their best ideas on youth empowerment. The activities included in each chapter are appropriate for communities that are new to building a foundation for youth empowerment, as well as for those already focused on youth empowerment goals.

Why the Emphasis on Empowerment Assets?

Thousands of Search Institute surveys of young people and adults reveal that the Empowerment assets "relate to the key developmental need youth [have] to be valued and valuable. They focus on [the] community['s] perception of youth (as reported by youth), and [on] opportunities for youth to contribute to society in meaningful ways."[1]

As a society, we can and must learn how to empower youth to contribute their considerable talents and gifts for the future benefit of all. Youth empowerment is a way of thinking about young people—a way that doesn't come naturally to many adults. It's embracing the fact that the teenage years don't have to be a time when we hold our breath to get through—it can be a time rich with opportunity. It's integrating the idea of youth empowerment into everyday existence and recognizing young people as vital members of society. It means asking yourself, every day, for every project, activity, duty, and program, the following questions:

How can I utilize young people in this effort?

How should I incorporate youth ideas into this project?

What questions should I ask youth before I begin?

How can I start with youth?

But it's not as easy as it sounds. Many youth feel devalued by the adults around them and report that their community doesn't provide useful roles for young people. Results from Search Institute's 2003 *Profiles of Student Life: Attitudes and Behaviors* survey show that just 22 percent of young people reported that their community values youth, while only 26 percent perceived that youth were given useful roles in their community. "It should become normative in all settings where youth are involved to seek their input and advice, to make decisions with them, and to treat them as responsible, competent allies in all asset-building efforts."

An organization or community that authentically seeks to empower its young people has an entirely different feel from one that does not. When youth are seen as partners in the decision making and implementation of programs that impact them, they can truly become part owners in the initiative. Young people benefit from an empowering environment because they're allowed to challenge themselves and spread their wings in a way that's not possible in a totally adult-led environment. And adults benefit from an end result that might never have been considered by an entirely adult-populated committee.

It's understood that youth see the world differently from adults—both in terms of the needs that exist and in how those needs can be addressed. The best environment mixes the two perspectives, valuing the reality and experiential base of adults and the creative optimism and energy of young people. Rebecca Grothe, author of *More Building Assets Together*, believes that "young people need to feel valued and valuable. This happens when they feel safe, when they believe that they are liked and respected, and when they make positive contributions to their families and communities."

The four Empowerment assets are interconnected in important ways. Each gains strength from the others. Here's one way to look at them:

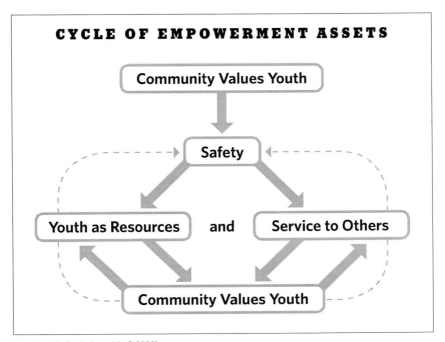

Figure by Kelly Curtis (copyright © 2008)

Young people are more likely to perceive that their community values them if they grow up in an environment that considers youth central and important to the community. This appreciative and supportive environment also works to provide a feeling of safety. When youth feel physically and psychologically safe, they can have the freedom, within boundaries, to become empowered as resources and through service. And as adults learn about the positive experiences of local youth, the community will come to value its youth even more. This perception, in turn, nurtures an environment that continues to promote safety, encourages youth to be resources of knowledge and skill, and encourages young people in service to others.

Relationship Building

"It is important that adults understand youth and treat us as equals. Age does not yield superiority; passion and love put everyone on an equal playing field. I think adults who don't stereotype youth and understand their intrinsic value to society are leaders who can make a difference."

—LISA SILVERMAN, 17, CENTENNIAL HIGH SCHOOL, ELLICOTT CITY, MARYLAND

Two basic concepts—building relationships and valuing the process over the product—create a base for all the Empowerment assets and enhance the strategies and theories you'll read about in the following chapters. Society tends to approach tasks at a pace that doesn't support the gradual work that asset building tries to accomplish. The need for efficiency eliminates many opportunities for a young person and an adult to build an authentic relationship around a task. John Ure, of the Heartwood Centre for Community Youth Development in Nova Scotia, says, "If the main focus is on relationship building—if the objective is development of the young person—then you'll approach the learning experience in a completely different way. You'll come to the task with a whole new attitude."

Measuring the presence and effects of relationship building between youth and adults in nonprogrammatic contexts does present some challenges. Programs often require immediate evidence of improvement, but trust takes time to build and cannot be rushed. Adults overlook this slow process in an effort to show results. However, in so many cases, the relationship itself is really the point. In dozens of interviews conducted with asset builders, one common behavior surfaced as critical to adults' efforts to empower youth: listening—with ears open, eyes meeting, and mouth closed.

Of course, relationship building is more than just listening, but adults who master this skill are halfway there. Excellent listeners are at the core of great adult and youth partnerships. The simplest human interactions—eye contact, a "hello," a friendly wave, and a smile—acknowledge that youth are important and worthy of our attention. As a society, we must meet youth where they are and find ways to stay with them on the journey. If we connect with them now, in simple yet significant ways, we'll face the future together with strength.

Process over Product

"What matters is the route taken, not the task at hand."

—JOHN URE, HEARTWOOD CENTRE FOR COMMUNITY YOUTH
DEVELOPMENT, HALIFAX, NOVA SCOTIA

Communities and organizations trying to reach youth often assume they have to implement a program, facilitate an activity, or create a project. But they forget that the most vital part is to make the program, activity, or project youth-centered. This means youth must be involved in every aspect of the process.

Sometimes the youth-adult partnership shouldn't focus on the end result. It's the act of fund-raising, not the dollars earned, and it's the journey, not the destination, that will be remembered. An adult may have performed the task a hundred times and be able to accomplish it with minimal effort, better and faster than a young person. But the task itself isn't necessarily the purpose of youth-adult collaboration. It's the learning and not the final score that is important.

The greatest challenge for most adults may be in learning to let go, allowing the project to take a different shape than planned and gradually giving up control over key components. Some adults need gentle encouragement to take the passenger seat once in a while. The secret is to trust youth to do the best job they can. Even when the product is imperfect, the process can be a beneficial learning experience for everyone.

Communities that embrace a philosophy of youth-adult partnerships may find it doesn't initially make life easier. Do empowered youth help solve problems quickly? Not always. Often, it's precisely the youth participation that complicates the process. And youth involvement on committees can lead to candid discussions and questions, which adults may not be prepared to field.

The truth is that our society feels less chaotic, less volatile, and less controversial when young people assume the role of silent sponges. Kids who sit at their desks, take notes, and don't ask for clarification make it easier for the traditional teacher to complete the lesson. Legislation delivered without youthful interruption or debate is more efficient. Children who follow the rules without questioning them cause less stress. But what are they learning? Will they later follow rules they had no part in establishing? Will they become critically thinking adults? Will they take the initiative to become courageous leaders?

Adults can gain immeasurable insight from youth if they make themselves available to discern it. Input that organizations receive from youth partners can improve communities in a way that nonempowering organizations cannot. It's better to genuinely ask for youth input and end up veering off the planned route than to play it safe and never take that step. You may run the risk of an end result that is flawed in some way, but the greater likelihood is that the outcome will be more effective when both youth and adults participate together.

One way to look at the side-by-side nature of youth empowerment is to view it as a three-legged seat. Each leg of the seat represents a vital aspect of true empowerment.

Figure by Kelly Curtis (copyright © 2008)

- **See Youth.** Youth all over the world have the potential to become empowered individuals, but only those who have *opportunities* will reach their full potential. Sometimes that opportunity presents itself in the form of an organization's mission, available funding, relevant programming, or an identified community need. But, as is often the case, an opportunity may originate with a single young person.

- **Teach Youth.** The next leg of the empowerment model is *skill*. Without it, highly motivated young people flounder in frustration as their efforts are wasted—in the wrong way, at the wrong time, with the wrong people. Youth need skills to enable them to make their ideas a reality—to experience success. Necessary skills for empowered youth include the elements of excellent communication: knowledgeable networking, effective public speaking, clear writing, etiquette savvy, knowledge of protocol, fund-raising ability, familiarity with technology, and all-around resourcefulness.

- **Believe in Youth.** The final leg of the empowerment model takes the longest to build—*trust*. Youth with opportunities and skills still need adults to trust them enough to gradually let go so that they can do what they're destined to do. Letting go does not come naturally to most adults and often requires a leap of faith.

Every time you help young people by offering them your trust, teaching them skills, and offering them opportunities, the empowerment process becomes easier and more effective and the possibilities become more exciting. You simply want to keep going.

The Freedom Writers Diary, written by novice American teacher Erin Gruwell and her 150 public school students, inspired a nation. Gruwell taught a group of at-risk first-year high school students. Over the course of four years, she empowered them to take control of their lives and transform themselves into forward-thinking, tolerant, inspired college students. Their story became the basis for the movie *Freedom Writers*.

Television talk-show host Oprah Winfrey established the Oprah Winfrey Leadership Academy for Girls in South Africa for talented girls in grades 7 through 12 from impoverished backgrounds. There, they gain leadership skills that will prepare them to become their country's future leaders. Imagine the potential impact these youth will have on their communities, their countries, and the world.

Of course, these are extraordinary examples of empowerment—most of us will never be the subject of a movie or the beneficiary of a public personality. But no matter how many stories we hear about resilient youth, remarkable survival, or inspirational courage, the catalyst is always the same: a caring adult.

When Mary Patterson, executive director of Project Cornerstone in San Jose, California, begins her asset training sessions with adults eager to learn more about empowering youth, she asks participants to think back to an experience, opportunity, or relationship they had as a child that helped them be successful or overcome adversity. She says, "People never recall the bicycle, but who taught them to ride it. They don't recall the basketball game, but who taught them to play it. They don't recall the English class, but who taught the lesson."

Be the *who*.

WHEN A COMMUNITY VALUES YOUTH

"[Empowerment is] not a bricks and mortar kind of thing. It is an atmosphere that transcends place. It's a way of interacting—a smiling face, a word of encouragement, a listening ear, a question or two that leads a young person to find a solution to his or her own problem."

—PAULA MORRIS, FOUNDER AND PRESIDENT OF KIDS OF HONOR, INC.

In 2006, Mayor Jeff Jacobs represented St. Louis Park, Minnesota—named one of "100 Best Communities for Young People" in 2005 and 2007 by the America's Promise Alliance, a national youth advocacy collaborative—at the annual America's Promise conference in Washington, D.C. He told the inspiring story of Sarah, a St. Louis Park teenager who overcame substantial odds to improve her life circumstances.

Sarah came from a troubled home that provided her with no parental guidance or support. She sometimes lived out of her car. Still, this resilient young woman cared for her younger sister, earned decent grades, and volunteered with younger kids. Elderly neighbors took her in, and community members supported her in whatever ways they could. When the Chamber of Commerce chose end-of-the-year scholarship recipients from among its high school graduates, Sarah was given the most prestigious award—for $5,000.

The Chamber invited scholarship winners and their families to a formal luncheon at which the scholarship winners would be given their awards. Unfortunately, Sarah's mother arrived inebriated and left before Sarah had accepted her scholarship. Sarah took the departure in stride—this was not an atypical occurrence in her life.

As the scholarship winners filed forward one at a time, family members applauded their daughters and sons, their nieces and neighbors. When it came time for Sarah to accept her award, a mob of 20 or more stood up and cheered. Community members had heard that she had won the university scholarship, and they attended the luncheon to support her. Business professionals took time away from their offices. Teachers and administrators left school for the occasion. Neighbors attended, too, because Sarah was important to them. They were her family.

And the happy outcome? Sarah's now a pharmacy student at the University of Minnesota.

Sarah's story need not be unique—communities can have this kind of impact on youth in similar situations. Mayor Jacobs' advice is simple but powerful: "Create a story like that. Engage the kids in your community to help you create stories like that. Those stories will find you."

Heirs to the Globe

"Kids are our best source of adults. If we don't train them, we'll run out. You have to give them the necessary resources and skills they need to operate the processes that they will one day inherit."

—MAYOR JEFF JACOBS, ST. LOUIS PARK, MINNESOTA

The way we guide young people today will ultimately determine the world's fate—and our own. But valuing the contributions of youth to our society—viewing youth as worthy of adult respect—is a relatively new concept. If the efforts of passionate individuals can create inroads toward youth-centered communities, then we can move toward inclusion of those who are arguably our most valuable resource. When youth speak of being valued, they mean that adults listen to them; take time to be with them; offer them leadership opportunities to speak out about issues that are important to them; and recognize them as assets to the community.

Community mobilization is vital to asset development in general, and central to asset 7: Community Values Youth in particular. Most caring adults would agree that a community that values its young people is more likely to create an environment that is emotionally and physically safe for them and prepared to use them as resources and service providers to the community. But "valuing youth" encompasses more than just making young people a focus in the community—it's empowering them to contribute as well.

See Youth, Hear Youth, Know Youth

"[Working to empower youth is something that drives you] from your core, your soul, and your being; it's a powerful spark from within that allows you to start the fire within someone else. I think adults become leaders because of [their] compassion. They care about others and want to improve the quality of life, . . . make a difference, and have a lasting impact."

—LISA SILVERMAN, 17, CENTENNIAL HIGH SCHOOL, ELLICOTT CITY, MARYLAND

At the heart of communities are *individuals*. Wisconsin high school principal Wayne Whitwam recalls the afternoon he stopped Jay, a fourth-year student, just before leaving school for the day. On his way out, Whitwam usually saw Jay and his girlfriend walking together. On this particular day, Jay was alone. In passing, Whitwam asked Jay where she was.

Jay looked down and muttered, "We broke up." A moment later, Jay asked Whitwam, "Got a minute?"

This brief, near miss turned into a two-hour conversation between the two in Whitwam's office. Jay ultimately revealed that he was think-ing of suicide. Whitwam was able to be present at a crucial moment in time for his student, and called Jay's mother, who came immediately to the school to see Jay safely home. Jay needed support that day, and his principal knew him well enough to recognize that need and lend him an attentive ear.

WHAT VALUE DOES YOUR COMMUNITY PLACE ON ITS YOUTH?

The following attitudes and behaviors characterize a community that values its youth. Take a moment to ask yourself how your community, school, or organization is doing when it comes to valuing its children and teens.

ALWAYS SOMETIMES NEVER

☐ ☐ ☐ Adults take the time to listen to and solicit feedback from young people.

☐ ☐ ☐ Adults see the strengths in youth more than they see problems and limitations.

☐ ☐ ☐ Youth identify places in the community where they feel appreciated and welcomed.

☐ ☐ ☐ Our community sponsors events designed especially for youth and families.

☐ ☐ ☐ Parents seek out opportunities to know, appreciate, and affirm their kids' friends.

☐ ☐ ☐ Adults (in addition to parents) attend kids' school plays, science fairs, athletic events, concerts, and other youth-centered community events.

☐ ☐ ☐ Adults talk to youth about their future careers, volunteer activities, and hobbies.

☐ ☐ ☐ Adults give youth positive feedback for doing a job well.

☐ ☐ ☐ The local newspaper celebrates the ways youth contribute to the community.

☐ ☐ ☐ Local businesses display youth artwork and promote youth extracurricular opportunities.

☐ ☐ ☐ Adults support and value the people who work with youth.

☐ ☐ ☐ Adults know and greet neighborhood children and adolescents by name.

☐ ☐ ☐ Employers develop family-friendly policies and opportunities for employees to connect with youth.

☐ ☐ ☐ Schools make it a priority to become caring environments and offer youth numerous opportunities for cocurricular activities.

☐ ☐ ☐ Local citizens allocate resources for the highest-quality school and youth programs.

Reprinted with permission from *Empowering Youth: How to Encourage Young Leaders to Do Great Things*, by Kelly Curtis, M.S. Copyright © 2008 by Search Institute, Minneapolis, Minnesota, 800-888-7828, www.search-institute.org. All rights reserved.

Adults who value youth *see youth, hear youth, and know youth*.

A community that values youth is composed of individual adults who make it their priority to acknowledge and care for young people. Teachers know students' names and use them consistently as they ask students for their opinions or inquire how the game went last night. Neighbors share with each other the good news they're hearing about kids on the block. Parents make a point of swapping supervisory responsibilities to provide fun and safe weekend gatherings for their children. Faith communities offer youth programming, and supporters fill the event bleachers, even during a losing season.

And a community that values youth consistently looks for ways to include its young people. Schools and recreation programs offer youth activities year-round. City planners seek youth input for projects that affect young people. Community celebration organizers design age-appropriate activities to engage young people and families. Community life at its best embraces all ages.

Building a Foundation

"If you expect a lot from youth, more often than not I believe they will step up to the plate. At the same time, be aware of [their] time constraints and lack of experience."

—DANIEL GILLESPIE, YALE UNIVERSITY STUDENT AND FORMER
MEMBER OF ALASKA'S SPIRIT OF YOUTH ORGANIZATION

Society's attitudes toward youth erect tall barriers to empowerment. And media outlets perpetuate the view that adolescence is primarily a time of peer pressure and risky behaviors. Many adults see media messages as evidence confirming that young people need to be protected and controlled, rather than regarded as competent and worthy of working collaboratively with adults. In a recent survey, only 21 percent of adults expressed confidence that youth can represent their community on a city council, and even fewer believed youth can organize and successfully carry out a community service project or serve as voting members of the school board.[1] We have our work cut out for us.

Possibly our greatest contribution as adults seeking to influence community attitudes is not spoken or written, but, rather, modeled. You may already be a convert to this view. Maybe you've witnessed some level of youth empowerment, and its potential impact on society piques your interest. Or you may stand firmly in the middle, understanding that communities must provide services to help young people, but you don't quite buy into the idea that youth and adults can partner in the deal. To change the attitudes of adults who aren't directly involved with positive youth development—some of whom may even see youth as problems to be solved—we need to be proactive.

Writers often live by the motto "show—don't tell." The reader should be able to "see" a scene unfold through the writer's skillful use of dialogue and description. As a result, the reader can interpret ideas without narrative interference from the author.

Likewise, in order for adults in the community to value their youth, they must be *shown* how to value youth—how to listen to youth, how to utilize youth strengths, how to interact with youth, how to appreciate youth. This means we have to practice and promote what we preach.

If we want youthful views to be represented on our community committees, we must ask for those same views to be expressed to our own organization's committees. If we want school policy makers to incorporate youth-centered values into school vision statements and goals, we must ask youth to identify their values for our own vision statements and goals. If we want adult service organizations to understand how youth might participate in their programming and projects, we must facilitate that same level of youth participation in our own programs and projects.

Your personal interactions with young people will serve as their training ground for every role you'd like to see them eventually assume in society. When you're given the opportunity to take a group of adults one step closer to effecting youth empowerment, you already have an empowered and experienced team of young people, prepared to communicate their views to adult committee members and policy makers and co-lead in-service workshops and trainings.

Each time Julia Hampton, coordinator of the Windham County Youth Initiative in Vermont, presents a youth project or leads an asset training session with adults, she does so with a well-trained youth partner. Julia knows that community members learn by seeing young people taking active and important roles. Hampton encourages youth and adult partners to co-lead civic group presentations and to discuss ways adults can support young people. She says, "Lead by example. Youth are capable, youth have a voice, and youth are resources in the community. Bring them along and have them be a part. Listen to their ideas."

When other adults can witness youth in action—as competent, confident citizens with their own reasonable opinions—a new frame of reference emerges for many. Each time adults see young people in this light, they're more likely to view youth as holding a possible solution to problems—as assets to the community.

A key focus for adult training opportunities can be good communication. Hampton says, "People don't realize what an impact they can have to just be friendly and make eye contact." Smiling at kids and greeting them—these are the most basic of human interactions. Yet we often overlook their importance. Simple actions change perception.

Spin, Baby, Spin! Designing a Public Relations Campaign

"Community Values Youth—Kids perceive that adults in the community value young people."

—EXCERPTED FROM *WHAT KIDS NEED TO SUCCEED*

The word "perceive" is critical to this asset definition because youth and adults often misunderstand each other. This asset requires youth to perceive that adults see them as valuable. But communication can easily break down between generations, so youth may underestimate the presence of adults who value them. For instance, within the same family siblings often perceive the same event differently. And parents' perceptions vary as well. Think of the teenager who comes home past curfew. Parents use a stern tone of voice and deliver a consequence. The teenager's perception? "My parents are mad and being mean to me." The parents' perception? "We're concerned for our teenager and want her or him to be safe." It logically follows that perceptions in the community might be inaccurate as well.

Oddly enough, the same misperceptions that impede communication between generations can actually improve community discussions. Youth insights can enrich adult conversations and strengthen communities that learn to act on them effectively. It's important that we don't assume we understand what youth are thinking. Parents can't assume their children know they are loved. Teachers can't assume students understand that teachers are proud of them when students work hard. Neighbors can't assume youth know when they're in the stands witnessing their mighty efforts. In some ways, shaping perception isn't much different from the "Mars and Venus" approach to relationships. We need to effectively communicate what we see, feel, do, and need.

Every year, businesses direct billions of marketing dollars toward shaping public perception. And just like businesses, communities need to create public relations plans to spin positive perceptions of youth and adults in their communities. Sound far-fetched? It's not.

We don't need to read "spin" as a four-letter word. After all, we're not planning to spin falsehoods or tell lies about the way adults feel about youth. We're not inventing events that didn't occur, and we're not promoting useless products to sell to the masses. We're spinning the *truth*. And we're making positive examples of the young, asset-rich members of our society.

Although it's embarrassing to admit, oftentimes what we know about the lives of teenagers and younger children is only what we see portrayed on television—or learn about them in magazines, newspapers, posters, meetings, school newsletters, and on cable channels and bulletin boards. Public relations plays a more vital role in our lives than we care to admit. A community that is critical of youth needs to see and hear good news promoting reasons to value youth. Society is filled with adults who want to believe the best about young people, but who need to see the evidence. They need to be taught what's right about youth. So, like it or not, in order for young people to understand that their community values youth, we need to embrace a PR plan and spin perception.

Create Positive Perceptions of Youth

"If I sit down and listen to them, I'll find a whole new side. Youth want people to get to know them and listen to what they have to say, not judge [them] on appearance."

—JULIA HAMPTON, COORDINATOR, WINDHAM COUNTY (VERMONT) YOUTH INITIATIVE

The residents of Windham County, Vermont, implemented a community assessment that revealed that people didn't necessarily believe it was their responsibility to support young people or even be nice to them on the street. As a strategy to engage the whole community, United Way hired a public relations professional to develop a campaign called "Help Empower Youth." The campaign focused on improving community perceptions of youth in the county by educating residents about the 40 Developmental Assets and putting into everyday language what people could do to build them.

Those involved in the media campaign identified various ways people could get information about young people—from radio, TV, newspapers, community presentations, bumper stickers, and mailings—and developed a multifaceted plan to disseminate positive youth publicity. This campaign educated the entire community, rather than the select few already aware of the good news about youth.

Newspapers are often more than willing to publish a series of articles on a topic of local interest, as long as staff aren't responsible for writing them. The savvy community asset builder recruits youth writers. They seek out news in the community, use their connections, and serve as positive journalists who celebrate youth accomplishments.

"How come when one of us does something wrong, you hear about it for weeks, but if we do something right, no one *ever* hears about it?" (from a youth participant at a Spirit of Youth "Speak Out" forum). Since 1997, the Spirit of Youth media project in Anchorage, Alaska, has addressed this typical youth concern, along with the overall negative image adults have of teenagers, by featuring hundreds of positive stories about Alaska youth on statewide television and radio, and in local newspapers.

Each month, residents, businesses, school boards, and teachers nominate hardworking and inspiring teenagers for their wide range of accomplishments and positive contributions to the community.

Spirit of Youth Teen Action Council members review nominations and choose one example for media spotlight and recognition.

Spirit of Youth cofounder Becky Judd says, "By getting these stories to the media, we are changing the perception of teenagers from troublemakers to problem-solvers. Anonymous phone surveys and evaluations have shown that after hearing repeated positive stories about youth, adults have more positive perceptions about youth."

Youth also learn journalism skills, conduct research, and provide a youth perspective on topics of interest on a monthly radio show as part of the Alaska Teen Media Institute. The institute functions as a teen newsroom where youth work as reporters, editors, and producers, under the guidance of an experienced journalist. Some of their stories have even been broadcast nationally and have won awards in journalism competitions against adults. Judd says that the teen media project "helps adults better understand youth perspective."

The typical youth project coordinator or participant is busy—and modest. Even if organizers have time to publicize their media initiative, some think it will look as though they're arrogant for suggesting that an accomplishment is newsworthy. But the purpose of publicity isn't for the benefit of the youth or adults involved in the activity— it's to educate members of the community who don't have direct, positive interactions with youth. And it's our responsibility to promote the good news about youth and youth programming, because while we notice asset-rich youth every day, we can't assume others do.

GET WRITING!

Start with these newspaper column ideas for getting the word out to local media outlets:

- Uncover little-known stories about young people's contributions in the community.
- Focus on youth service projects initiated both locally and far away.
- Highlight leadership opportunities available to youth through community organizations.
- Recognize citations and honors awarded to local young people.
- Spread the good news about youth beyond the football score and honor roll!

PUBLICITY CHANNELS

Try these publicity avenues for getting the word out to the community at large. Don't be concerned if you're not a professional writer. Simple, direct language is all that is required.

- Columns in community and school newspapers
- School newsletters and e-mail communications
- Community education bulletins
- Public service announcements on local TV stations and public access cable channels
- Radio station programming, promotions, and public service announcements
- Direct mail campaigns or tip sheets included in utility bills
- Bumper stickers
- Local business window stickers
- Web logs (blogs)
- Refrigerator magnets
- Brochures
- Youth and adult partner presentations introducing assets to civic groups

Spin Supportive Perceptions about *Adults*

"Always see the potential that lies within every kid.
We all have something inside of us, but if no one sees it,
then we are less likely to harness that potential and
use it. Adults should know we look up to them for advice
and constructive criticism."

—ASHLEY PRATTE, 17, MANCHESTER, 2006 NEW HAMPSHIRE HONOREE,
PRUDENTIAL SPIRIT OF COMMUNITY AWARDS

The same philosophy that emphasizes the importance of publicizing youth accomplishments holds true when spinning perceptions about adults. A community might employ a first-class public relations plan for educating adults about the great things youth do. A majority of adults may hold an excellent opinion of youth and participate in activities that empower and build assets in youth. And the youth directly involved with these adults understand that the community values them. But many youth are *not* involved with these adults or programs, and, therefore, don't share the same perception. We can't assume they've met *any* adult asset builders. Communities need to publicize programs well and create opportunities relevant to the children who benefit from them the most. Positive publicity helps foster the notion that the community cares about them.

The residents of Charlotte County, New Brunswick, Canada, organized an eight-part series of newspaper articles featuring local asset-building champions. The series profiled ordinary adults who were making extraordinary contributions to the lives of youth. The publicity reflected a solid foundation of support that exists for young people in Charlotte County. A by-product of promoting asset building by adults is that other adults learn how to become involved as asset builders, and they understand that asset-building actions are not only acceptable but even *expected*.

Many actions improve communication and understanding between youth and adults: joint participation on municipal advisory groups, at youth rallies, on youth center advisory boards, and through other mechanisms that seek youth input. But *personal* interactions between youth and adults may make the most effective impact on youth opinions about adults.

An Alaska Spirit of Youth survey indicated it was the way *business owners*, rather than teachers, family members, and neighbors, treated young people that profoundly influenced whether or not youth felt valued in their community. Each year the Alaska Spirit of Youth organization honors those businesses that hire youth, prepare them for future careers, and treat teenage customers with respect. The Teen Action Council regularly reviews nominations for this honor. Businesses that meet the criteria are awarded a "Youth-Friendly Business" window logo sticker, along with local media recognition and endorsement.

Daniel Gillespie, a former Spirit of Youth Teen Action Council member, remembers when the council was initially approached about creating a new program to make businesses more responsive and youth-friendly. Gillespie says:

What I didn't realize was [that our adult contact] was not coming to tell us how this program would work—[she was coming to] ask us how we could make it work. After several meetings, our ideas turned into a coherent and detailed new statewide project . . . The program is very much youth-led, the criteria were developed by youth, and youth are the ones who implement the program, from making decisions on deciding who qualifies [for the "Youth-Friendly Business" award] to doing the actual presentation of the award. This was the first time I had been part of the creation of something [like this program], rather than just [carrying out] the execution [of the idea].

A good public relations campaign serves many purposes. It generates support for youth. It changes the attitudes of adults. It modifies youth perceptions of adults. Spin is a good thing, as long as it moves your community in the right direction.

ACTIVITY 1

Brainstorm a Campaign to Publicize Good News about Youth

Audience: Adults and youth in community settings.

Focus: Brainstorm ways to publicize the good news about youth and adult asset builders.

You will need: Room, tables and chairs set up for groups of six to eight, flipchart paper, and markers for each table. Invite a youth to cofacilitate the activity.

Before the group arrives: Write various public relations idea starters on your flipchart paper, suggesting the many ways to send information to the public: through media outlets, e-mail, regular mail, through groups and individuals. If table groups are a mix of youth and adults, ensure that youth are seated in pairs.

Set the stage: Explain that communities benefit from a positive public relations plan just as corporations do. The purpose of this campaign is to educate members of the community who don't have direct, positive interactions with youth. It's the responsibility of all group members to promote the good news about youth and youth programming.

Step 1: Show the participants your idea starters. Ask them to use the markers and flipchart paper to record ways they could spread positive news about youth. Groups should organize their ideas based on your idea starters. Explain that in the brainstorming process, there is no criticism—it's a free flow of ideas that shouldn't be fine-tuned until later. Encourage participants to consider small and big ways to publicize. Sometimes it's the simplest strategies that have the greatest impact.

Step 2: Allow the brainstorming process to continue as long as ideas flow. Then ask participants to fine-tune their lists, circling the most viable ideas, based on group commitment, available budget and resources, and the idea's effectiveness. Groups should also choose a slogan for their campaign.

Step 3: Ask each group to share its campaign slogan and key ideas with the larger group.

Reflection Questions:

- What "good news" did you learn today that you didn't already know about youth in your community?
- Did you discover any simple ways to integrate good news about youth into your role in the community?
- Which community members will learn the most from your campaign?

ACTIVITY 2

Signs of Support

Audience: Neighbors, creative parents, and other community sign makers.

Focus: Support local youth who are embarking on special efforts—extracurricular, academic, or service-related.

You will need: Flipchart paper or whiteboard, marker, poster board, paintbrushes, sign paint, water, newspaper (to protect the paint area), sturdy tape, and yard stakes for displaying signs.

Before the group arrives: Identify the youth effort that will be the focus of your campaign of support. It could be a sports team competing at a state tournament, a group of students preparing for achievement testing, artists displaying their work at a community show, or a youth ministry group embarking on a mission trip. Write sample slogans—"Go for it, Jenny!" or "We're behind you, Scott!"—on flipchart paper or a whiteboard, and prepare a complete list of youth names and neighbors to be included. Let participants know they should "dress down" for the painting activity.

Set the stage: Discuss the competition or event, and the key details that could be included on signs to encourage community members to attend (date, time, and location).

Step 1: Show participants your sample slogans, and ask for more ideas. Ask people to sign up for youth names until all youth are "claimed." Encourage sign painters to create their signs using the brainstormed slogans, event details, and names of youth they're supporting.

Step 2: Hang signs to dry while participants create more. Encourage participants to chat and get to know each other while they paint signs.

Step 3: Supply painters with tape and sign stakes to prepare the signs for posting. Have painters divide the signs among themselves, and encourage them to ask their neighbors to display the supportive signage in their yards.

Reflection Questions:

- What special efforts by youth were you unaware of prior to this activity?
- How do you think community members will react when they see these signs? How will youth react?
- Who could we invite to join in with supportive signage in the future?

(Activity adapted with permission from Children First, St. Louis Park, Minnesota.)

ACTIVITY 3

R-E-S-P-E-C-T

Audience: Young people, civic leaders, and other adult community members.

Focus: This activity offers adults an opportunity to understand how their actions and words can make youth in the community feel either respected and valued or undervalued and disregarded.

You will need: Index cards (two different colors) and a representative group of youth who meet with you prior to the adult meeting.

Before the adult group arrives: Prior to the day of the community presentation or training, gather a group of young people together to provide anonymous feedback to the community. Distribute one index card (all one color) to each young person. Ask youth to identify and describe a situation where they felt valued and respected by an adult in the community. Next, distribute another index card (of a different color) to each person, and ask youth to identify and describe a situation where they felt disregarded and undervalued by adults in the community. Youth should be as detailed as possible when explaining the situation, but they shouldn't mention names. Suggest that they look at the activity as "telling a story." The more specific their story, the more effective they will be in teaching adults. Collect the index cards, choose three to five examples of each situation, and remove names for complete anonymity. Consider selecting the most representative stories—examples most of your audience will be able to relate to. Thank youth for their participation.

Set the stage: At the adult meeting, explain that sometimes adults don't realize just how much their words and actions do make an impression on youth. Youth and adult perceptions of the same event may vary a great deal. Remind participants that all people (including youth) need to be treated with respect.

Step 1: Read selected stories aloud to adults, first mentioning examples of times when youth felt disrespected. Ask participants if they've ever witnessed a similar situation. Ask participants how they would feel if someone treated them in this way.

Step 2: Read aloud examples of times when youth felt respected. Ask participants how they would feel if someone treated them in this way.

Step 3: Distribute cards containing examples of disrespectful treatment to small groups of participants. Each group should brainstorm how they think the situation could have been handled differently. Ask groups to share their ideas with the larger group.

Reflection Questions:

• What youth situations surprised you most?

• Did you find yourself remembering times when you may have caused similar feelings in young people—both respect and disrespect?

• How can you help generate awareness of a need for intentional, respectful treatment of young people among fellow community members?

(Activity adapted with permission from Project Cornerstone, Santa Clara County, California.)

Create a Utopian Community

A new skateboard ramp graces the neighborhood park and buzzes with activity. "Vote YES!" signs reflect evidence of a recently passed school referendum. Volunteers staff creative, energy-filled after-school programs. Local business owners and youth speak with mutual respect—and genuine interest—about the leadership conference they attended together. A group of racially, socially, and economically diverse teenagers walks into the city hall to attend a youth commission meeting. An 18-year-old county board member meets with an adult colleague to research an environmental issue they plan to present to the public. Youth and adult members of a summer carnival committee work side by side to design a community celebration that engages young people as well as adults. A "wall of achievement" featuring names of young leaders recognizes not just the best of the best, but the best part of each person.

This ideal community values its youth. Is this a utopia? Perhaps. Certainly, it's a collage of actual asset-rich communities, all of which value youth. Communities with solid foundations of positive attitudes toward young people are more likely to embrace progressive strategies for youth empowerment. Each community boasts its own unique strengths and weaknesses, history and champions, initiatives and programs. Evaluation of a community's assets can reveal which strategies can be implemented most effectively. And not all communities that demonstrate utopian qualities necessarily start this way.

Youth–Adult Partnerships: Lead, Empower, and Get Out of the Way!

"[Empowerment] is having confidence because someone has spoken it into you."

—JULIA HAMPTON, WINDHAM COUNTY YOUTH INITIATIVE COORDINATOR

Watch any effective coach in action, and you'll witness empowerment. Think about reality TV programming. Whether the coaching focuses on weight loss, better parenting, or building a corner shelf, you'll see the same thing—demonstration, instruction, encouragement, and celebration.

This is no different from methods used by adults who coach youth—it's about empowerment and participation. A side-by-side youth and adult partnership generates the best results—adults who recognize youth strengths and encourage them in that direction. The challenge is to figure out how to empower youth to be the "change agents." When youth recognize and voice a need for change, they are best served when adults walk alongside them as youth take steps to make change happen.

Climbing the Ladder of Participation

"It's important for adults to understand where they really and honestly are in terms of believing that young people can be resources. That's the first step."

—CINDY CARLSON, DIRECTOR, HAMPTON COALITION FOR YOUTH, HAMPTON, VIRGINIA

Sometimes communities only give lip service to the notion of valuing youth. Young people may believe they've been given a voice in their community because they've earned roles of perceived importance, when in fact the title is a sham and they haven't actually been given a voice at all. This "tokenism"—creating a false appearance of inclusive practices (intentional or not)—limits the participation of a minority group (young people, in this case). This practice demeans young people, denying them productive decision-making roles in an organization and frustrating adult asset builders who hope to showcase youth talent.

Children's Environments Research Group codirector Roger Hart, a developmental psychologist at the City University of New York, has developed what he calls the "Ladder of Participation" to illustrate degrees of community inclusion and collaboration with regard to youth and adult partnerships. Manipulation, decoration, and tokenism define the lower (discriminatory) rungs of the ladder, while rising above them are the organization's developing levels of youth inclusion on the ladder's higher rungs. The terminology used to define each rung makes strong statements about the levels of group inclusion experienced by youth.

The truth may be that many organizations must transition through some of the lower-level rungs or stages along the Ladder of Participation before they can fully embrace the idea that communities indeed benefit from youth participation and leadership. Often, an organization is simply unprepared to integrate youth into the way it operates. Even members with the best intentions may stereotype and dismiss critical remarks from youth when they are offered, since such views may differ from the current course of action. Without training, members might misunderstand the role of youth in their organization, and young people's developmental ability to handle sophisticated situations. Some adults may even feel they were forced into a partnership without seeing any benefit.

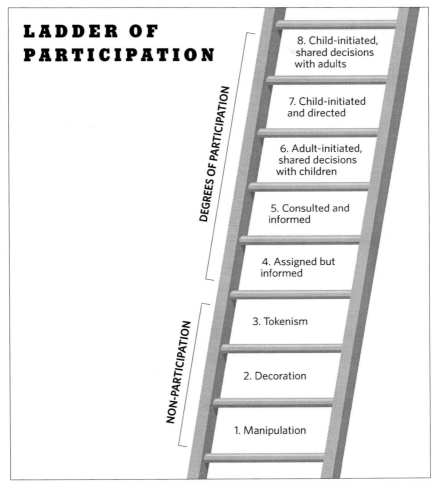

LADDER OF PARTICIPATION

DEGREES OF PARTICIPATION

8. Child-initiated, shared decisions with adults

7. Child-initiated and directed

6. Adult-initiated, shared decisions with children

5. Consulted and informed

4. Assigned but informed

NON-PARTICIPATION

3. Tokenism

2. Decoration

1. Manipulation

Reproduced by permission of the publisher from Hart, Roger A., "Children's Participation: From Tokenism to Citizenship," Florence: UNICEF International Child Development Centre, 1992 (Innocenti Essay 4).

Strong adults are needed to guide a group through the process of incorporating youth leadership, and even stronger youth are needed to withstand the change. Like saying "no" to peer pressure, it's difficult to stand firm on your convictions when surrounded by people who don't understand you.

Ideally, youth will serve as full-fledged voting members of a community board, committee, or team. But realizing this goal may take time. Perhaps an adult group isn't quite ready for that leap, or logistical issues such as transportation, communication, work schedules, and extracurricular responsibilities prevent youth inclusion. Perhaps youth aren't prepared to be effective members of the committee. Maybe the youth member doesn't freely share her opinions with the group as she does among her peers.

But with time and commitment, organizations can learn to mesh adult and youth strengths. "It can be just as scary for an adult to let a young person take on responsibility as it is for the young people themselves to do so. Having [previously] agreed-upon and clearly articulated ideas and goals contributed by both parties certainly makes that huge leap more comfortable for everyone involved," says Pat Howell-Blackmore of Thrive! The Canadian Centre for Positive Youth Development.

Youth as Stakeholders

"Bite your tongues and listen—for every meeting you have with adult advisors, find a youth group to chat over the same issues. You'll be amazed at the positive flow of ideas."

—PAULA MORRIS, FOUNDER AND PRESIDENT OF KIDS OF HONOR

Communities can guide residents toward embracing youth inclusion by introducing young people as "stakeholders." The nonprofit community change organization United Way partnered with the residents of Leeds and Grenville, Ontario, Canada, to embark on a two-year town meeting project called Community Matters. In the initiative's first year, many stakeholders attended the town meetings and discussed important issues related to community vision and the status of young people that were so important to them. Unfortunately, children and youth did not participate in the discussions.

In the project's second year, the two communities organized another series of town hall meetings to solicit input from children and youth in grades 7 through 12. The meetings included 1,000 kids from 21 different schools. Gymnasiums served as meeting places where youth divided into small groups. Students interviewed each other about issues that mattered to them, and wrote responses on index cards (see Activity 6, page 42). Then the community followed up with a youth summit in which 200 young people addressed those identified issues in small groups and discovered solutions to their concerns.

Young people want to see the results of their efforts. David Huether, an adult volunteer for Every Kid in Our Communities of Leeds and Grenville, Ontario, Canada, says, "We reported [what we learned from the youth summit] to all municipal leaders, involved lots of politicians and community leaders, and established youth advisory committees." As a result, adults had a much greater understanding of what's important to youth in their communities.

Santa Clara County, California, organizes a similar opportunity for its youth stakeholders. The community holds an annual event for youth to talk to the mayor. It's a casual affair, with food, music, and fun. Mary Patterson, the executive director of Santa Clara County's Project Cornerstone asset-building initiative, says, "One year the event with Mayor Kelly might be called 'Kickin' It with Kelly.' The next year it might be 'Dish with Doolittle.' The format changes, but kids are [always] in charge, and no question is dumb."

Finding a Balance

"It isn't empowering to showcase young people and then talk about them, [rather than] allowing youth to talk for themselves. It's important [for adults] to learn the delicate balance of being supportive and then get out of the way."

—NANCY TELLETT-ROYCE, SEARCH INSTITUTE COMMUNITY LIAISON

People can be dissatisfied with the rate of change, even in asset-rich communities. The truth is, people need patience and persistence when trying to positively shape attitudes toward youth. The Coalition for Youth in Hampton, Virginia, created a model to help residents conceptualize youth engagement in the community called the Hampton Youth Civic Engagement Program. The program has been so successful that it was chosen from over 1,000 applicants for the prestigious 2005 Innovations in American Government Award from the Ash Institute for Democratic Governance and Innovation at Harvard University's Kennedy School of Government.

The coalition coordinates annual partnerships for 1,000 young people in a variety of settings: a neighborhood youth advisory board, teen advisory groups for parks and recreation, the superintendent's advisory group, and secondary school advisory teams. The program offers some youth the opportunity to create official documents and plans for the town. A group of 24 youth also comprises the city's Youth Commission and sits on other appointed committees throughout the city. And the coalition still doesn't believe it has the youth engagement process completely figured out!

Director Cindy Carlson says the Hampton model has centered on what youth empowerment really means—focusing on finding the balance between adult and youth responsibilities in an initiative. She says, "I see it as [requiring] a much deeper, fundamental change in the way adults view young people and the systems we perpetuate that disempower them."

So how did the Hampton community succeed in empowering its youth? The right mix of adult stakeholders—mayor, city management, superintendent, and police chief—was connected by the same fundamental beliefs from the very beginning. "They helped us to kick off in a way that people right away saw the value and could build on the momentum," says Cindy Carlson.

The Hampton Coalition for Youth featured longevity of a core group of people in positions that allowed them to influence others who, says Carlson, "are willing to struggle and work and be stubborn enough not to let it go . . . Youth rise to the occasion, any time they're called upon. They offer a constant stream of proof that the coalition is worthwhile, it works, and it's a valuable place for us to invest our resources." (For more information about the Hampton Coalition for Youth, see www.hampton.gov/foryouth.)

The coalition approaches its work in a systematic, extensive, and intentional way, but still continues to search for the perfect mix. A line separates adult guidance, control, and letting go of the reins—and the line moves, depending on the project. Early in the initiative, Carlson discovered that adults tend to fall on opposite ends of a continuum in their partnerships with youth. Those with a strong investment in the outcome tend to direct the work that's going on. At the other end of the spectrum are adults who want to sit back and exert no guidance or control over the partnership. They say, "It's their [the kids'] show—I don't want to intervene."

Neither of these extremes functions well in the coalition setting. They're simply not conducive to encouraging youth empowerment. Carlson says adults must learn to maintain a relationship with youth through mutual respect and accountability, to impart wisdom, and take charge when necessary, "but know when to let go to allow young people to drive the train."

Just as adults struggle to make the transition toward youth inclusion, youth also hesitate to take the leap. Even when working in groups of empowered young people, it's difficult for adults to move into this new relationship with youth. "Being a resource, a cocreator of the work, is just as challenging for young people. They've never been treated that way," Carlson says. While youth adjust, they may engage ineffectively in their work. Some may resort to saying only what they think adults want to hear, while others lose their grounding and wield their power too strongly. Carlson says, "For young people, it's a matter of finding . . . balance in the group so they feel comfortable in [their new] position."

There's no magic formula for creating the optimal youth-adult partnership. The parameters for this middle ground differ by mission, adult players, and developmental abilities of the youth involved. But adults who are naturally attuned to an individual's gifts can engage youth as powerful players in the project.

Youth as Resources

"Encourage youth leadership. Create a mechanism in your community to get youth voice on adult boards, [and] not just as window dressing. Have those boards meet after school hours. That's often the biggest hurdle."

—PAULA MORRIS, FOUNDER AND PRESIDENT OF KIDS OF HONOR

William Lofquist, an Arizona-based writer and longtime cheerleader for youth development, identifies three types of adult attitudes toward young people—as objects, as recipients, and as resources—that lie along a continuum. The Hampton community used Lofquist's ideas as it moved toward a model of youth empowerment. While most community organizations have steered away from viewing youth as objects, few truly embrace them as resources. It's commonly assumed that young people are recipients who benefit from a community's resources, and not the other way around.

SPECTRUM OF ADULT ATTITUDES TOWARD YOUNG PEOPLE

Style #1	Style #2	Style #3
Young people viewed as **OBJECTS**	Young people viewed as **RECIPIENTS**	Young people viewed as **RESOURCES**
• Adult is in control, with no intention of youth involvement.	• Adult is in control and allows youth involvement.	• Youth/adult partnership allows shared control.
• Objective is personal growth of young people.	• Objective is personal growth of young people.	• Objective is increased organizational effectiveness.
• By-product is conformity of young people and acceptance of the program as it is.	• By-product is increased organizational effectiveness.	• By-product is personal growth of young people and adults.

Reproduced by permission from William A. Lofquist, "The Spectrum of Adult Attitudes Toward Young People," *The Technology of Prevention Workbook*, 1989, 47–50.

Members of many youth-serving organizations believe adults know what is best for young people, so they allow youth to participate only because it's good for them. On the other hand, empowering groups view youth as resources to be mined, and believe youth and adults can share almost any leadership and decision-making role. This attitude requires an entirely different level of commitment. To be successful, young people and adults need to develop skills for shared leadership and decision making. Lofquist suggests that moving organizations to this level of youth empowerment can lead to multiple benefits, including increased organizational effectiveness and personal growth of youth and adults.

Whatever Works!

"There's a triangle of opportunity, from service to influence to shared leadership. In a community where young people are truly empowered, they would be active at those various levels. The mistake people make is thinking they all have to serve on the school board."

—CINDY CARLSON, DIRECTOR, HAMPTON COALITION FOR YOUTH, HAMPTON VIRGINIA

There's more than one way to benefit from including young people in planning and carrying out a community's priorities. Hampton's model of youth civic engagement defines three routes for effective youth participation:

- Projects, tasks, and service
- Input and consultation
- Shared leadership

The levels of youth participation increase in complexity and commitment, which results in attracting a rich and diverse pool of youth leaders from all areas of their community. Various inclusion methods exist, and effective communities determine which option works best in each area. Many communities give youth a voice through youth summits and youth commissions, while others ask youth to serve in full voting roles in local government. Sometimes a commission composed entirely of youth will more honestly discuss issues than it otherwise would in a mixed group of youth and adults. Youth subcommittees facilitate discussions about important youth issues, and then send a representative to share those findings with the adult decision-making board.

All organizations can do *something* to move in the direction of full youth participation. Like learning styles in children, "different" doesn't necessarily mean better or worse. Attitudes matter more than the system that's used for encouraging the youth participation. The standard is—whatever works.

Youth Summit

"[To feel empowered means] having someone to listen to my problems, and having the resources to solve my problems."

—SHAWN WILLIS, JR., 14, ST. LOUIS PARK, MINNESOTA,
SKATEBOARD PARK DESIGN TEAM MEMBER

When youth participate in civic affairs, they benefit tremendously. No one disputes that. And few service opportunities can top the title "city council member" as a résumé builder on a college application. But the community benefits as well. Having the youth perspective is a valuable tool that can only be gained by asking for it.

A group of teens in St. Louis Park, Minnesota, visited their city council to make a compelling case for renting a skatepark. The council agreed to their request and rented the equipment. Because of continual requests to design a permanent site for skateboarders, the city then sponsored a youth summit and invited youth to share their thoughts about various topics, including the establishment of a permanent skatepark. The youth summit invited city council, county board, and school board members, state representatives, social workers, police officers, public works officials, school staff, and parents.

But roles were reversed at this summit—youth would talk, while adults could only listen. Mayor Jeff Jacobs says, "If you had closed your ears, you would have stereotyped and discounted them. But if you closed your eyes and listened . . ."

The skateboard enthusiasts impressed adults with their respect and social responsibility. Youth confidently explained what they would like in a skatepark and why they would use it. They acknowledged that some business owners were uncomfortable with kids skating outside their establishments. The youth didn't want trouble—just a safe place to hang out with their friends, doing something they enjoyed.

Council members researched appropriate locations and the financial feasibility of the skatepark, and discussed the idea with the parks and recreation board, the neighborhood residents, regional walking and biking trail planners, and school personnel. The council devised a plan they were proud to implement, and finally asked for input one evening from those who some might consider the most important stakeholders—the young people who proposed the park.

The ensuing discussion revealed that the council's plan was overly elaborate. What local youth really wanted was a relatively simple skatepark with low ramps and few restrictions. The more sophisticated park planned by the council would require user fees and adult supervision because of higher ramps. The youth had also wanted the park to be located near the town's economic center because of its accessibility.

Mayor Jacobs says, "We realized we were on the exact right path to building them the exact skateboard park they didn't want. We stopped the presses. These kids changed history that night." From then on, youth participated until the park was completed. Adults sought out skating enthusiasts at the temporary park and asked them to become involved. Jacobs says some of the kids were drifters who had never really latched on to anything before in their lives. Their involvement in the skatepark project gave them a genuine feeling of importance.

Shawn Willis, Jr., served on the design team that made the park a reality. Metro television news reporters interviewed him. He greeted President George W. Bush when the president visited St. Louis Park and represented his community at a conference in Washington, D.C. Shawn says, "Without the support of my mom and other people in my community, I don't know where I would be. They support me in my efforts to become a success."

Simply listening to the stakeholders in this situation made the difference between success and failure. The St. Louis Park story has become one of the standards for public process—and a template used in council decision making—not just for youth but for the public in general.

Making Connections

"I was given opportunities to stand on stage with Al Gore and Colin Powell . . . the doors this opens for a 13- to 15-year-old! Those opportunities led to others I couldn't have imagined at the time."

—REBECCA JARVIS, CNBC TELEVISION BUSINESS CORRESPONDENT

Often, empowering organizations facilitate connections. Each group may have a separate goal, strength, purpose, and financial base—much like individuals do. But to promote and expand an atmosphere of empowerment, we need to empower residents and organizations in the same ways we empower youth. We identify strengths, provide training, and ask for help. We need to provide links between youth programs, schools, faith communities, and other organizations learning to engage youth. The role of go-between—matching up youth with the adult organizations that could assist youth, or benefit from youth participation—often is the critical piece that makes empowerment a reality.

Heartwood, a nonprofit organization in Halifax, Nova Scotia, focuses on social change, youth needs, and youth service. But it also meets a need in facilitating youth-adult partnerships. Most of its work is adult professional development contracted by organizations, communities, or government entities like public libraries. Heartwood trainers teach adults how to interact with youth and then facilitate a combined youth-adult in-service to practice effective interaction. Finally, Heartwood trainers encourage a discussion with young people about what the organization could do to better serve youth.

John Ure, Heartwood's associate director, says, "Most youth organizations focus on their service. They provide programming, but they're so busy and overwhelmed doing just that, that they can't do more. We do professional development with other service providers and get involved with 'systems change.'"

He says it can be a long process—first, professional development, then youth and leadership development, youth and adult partnerships, organizational development, and, finally, focusing on the way individuals go about their work. "Sooner or later [the process] changes the nature of relationships in the system."

There is power in connections. Communities in Schools (CIS) builds partnerships with kids across six school districts in Houston to encourage them to stay in school. CIS board member Pat Rosenberg had heard about a scholarship grant from the Houston Endowment to be used for youth participants who hoped to attend Search Institute's annual Healthy Communities•Healthy Youth (HC•HY) Conference. Rosenberg told CIS about the scholarship opportunity, and CIS invited its 106 member schools to nominate two busloads of Houston youth to attend the conference in Dallas. Included in the group were three youth, Ireoine, Nikata, and Nathan, who'd relocated to Houston and enrolled at Booker T. Washington High School after losing their homes to Hurricane Katrina.

The students were among those who received scholarship grants from the Houston Endowment to attend the conference. Afterward, these youth returned to Houston as changed individuals. They were able to move beyond their present-day challenges to adopt a "future" orientation. These teenagers wanted to make a difference in their community.

Rosenberg later campaigned for additional funding from the Houston Endowment so she could take 33 more youth to the HC•HY conference in Minneapolis the following year. And the three "Katrina" kids wanted to go again. Everyone could see what a difference the previous year's conference participation had made in them, so the CIS project manager found scholarships for the three, and Continental Airlines donated their plane tickets.

These three young people now live and breathe the positive orientation of the Developmental Assets. They started a group in Houston called Youth Taking Action. Ireoine wants to be an English teacher. Nikata is a student at the University of Houston. Rosenberg says that on the way home from the Minneapolis conference, Nathan remarked, "This was something good that happened from Hurricane Katrina. What would have happened to us if Katrina hadn't?"

Empowering Adults

"[Empowering adults] are able to trust that youth can and will be able to rise to the challenge; they see qualities or gifts in young people that can be encouraged, enhanced, and supported even if the youth do not yet see it themselves; they see what is possible, the 'what if' in each young person."

—PAT HOWELL-BLACKMORE, DIRECTOR OF COMMUNICATIONS & PROGRAMS, THRIVE! THE CANADIAN CENTRE FOR POSITIVE YOUTH DEVELOPMENT

So what does it take to build a community that values youth? It takes empowering, asset-building adults. It takes adults who value youth.

Your asset-building role may be as a teacher, facilitator, parent, or bus chaperone. It may be as a cheerleader of asset-building champions. It may be as a youth mentor or as a donor of money—in small or large quantities. It may be as a hotel manager who removes the sign prohibiting toys in the pool. It may be as one who stops at lemonade stands. In whatever empowering, asset-building role you serve, you're important. You're vital. All of you together connect to create a community that values youth.

ACTIVITY 4

"Youth as Leaders" Brainstorming

Audience: Adults involved in education, government, or other community settings.

Focus: Adults brainstorm ways youth can serve in leadership roles in a particular environment.

You will need: Room set up in table groups of six to eight, flipchart paper, and markers for each table. Invite a young person to share leadership of the activity. Reproduce the "Ladder of Youth Participation" (see page 29) as a handout.

Before the group arrives: On flipchart paper, compile a list of youth participation or leadership roles you've read or heard about, particularly those related to the type of organization that will participate in the brainstorming activity. Consider both minor and major roles to illustrate a range of opportunities for youth involvement.

Set the stage: Introduce the "Ladder of Youth Participation." Describe the significance of youth empowerment, and discuss ways it benefits young people and the organizations that empower them. Explain that anyone who works with youth has an opportunity to empower young people. Introduce the activity by explaining ways youth already participate and provide leadership in various communities. Discuss the list you compiled earlier.

Step 1: Ask participants to brainstorm the types of participation and leadership roles that youth could fill in adult organizations or within the community. Record their ideas on flipchart paper. Explain that in the brainstorming process, there is to be no criticism of suggestions—it's a free-flowing exchange of ideas that will be fine-tuned later. Encourage participants to think of small and large roles, as well as long-term and short-term commitments. Youth leadership comes in many forms.

Step 2: Allow the brainstorming process to continue as long as ideas flow freely. Then ask participants to organize the list by level of commitment and type of expectation. On a new sheet, each group should draw the "Ladder of Youth Partici-pation" and organize their favorite ideas on the appropriate rungs.

Step 3: Ask table groups to evaluate the lists and determine which youth roles would be most effective and feasible within their organization.

Step 4: As a large group, create an action plan for inviting youth into these new roles, and set up a timetable for putting the plan into action.

Reflection Questions:

• Which new ideas for youth leadership roles surprised you?

• What youth leadership roles did this process lead you to consider integrating into your daily activities? How might you do so?

• Who are the young people you think would be a great fit for one of the roles the group discussed?

ACTIVITY 5

What Do You Value?

Audience: Youth and adult community members.

Focus: To understand and appreciate the values critical to youth, and to compare them to values critical to adults.

You will need: Scissors and handouts for each participant.

Before the group arrives: Arrange room by table groups, seating youth and adults together at each table. Place scissors and handouts on each table (one per person). Create a "values" handout (printed with 30 "values" in large, evenly spaced type), which includes words and expressions that are meaningful in your community (for instance, honesty, academic achievement, financial success, happiness, stability, adventure, peace, worship, integrity, diversity, safety, education, cleanliness, hard work, accomplishment, acceptance, independence, organization, generosity, com-munity, competition, friendship, order, social justice, conservation, health, family time, pride, helpfulness, frugality).

Set the stage: Misunderstandings between adults and youth are common, because each group comes into a situation with a unique perspective and experience. It is normal for personal values to change with time and experience. But we also tend to make fixed assumptions about what other groups may think, feel, believe, and want. This exercise is designed to identify and explain what matters to each of us. It is criti-cal that participants not judge responses offered during this exercise. Explain to the group that this gathering must feel safe in order for all to share thoughts freely. The group won't be debating values, just naming and defining them.

Step 1: Participants cut out the 30 values on the handout, and choose 12 that best describe their own personal values. Place discarded values in a center pile.

Step 2: When everyone has narrowed their lists to 12, ask participants to prioritize their values, keeping just their top five.

Step 3: Within table groups, have youth and adult participants take turns sharing their top five values with each other, defining what they believe each value means to them.

Reflection Questions:

- Which youth or adult values surprised you, and why?
- In general, what were the top values chosen by youth? Chosen by adults? How might these choices affect youth/adult communication?
- What can we all do to understand and appreciate each other's values?

(Activity adapted with permission from Camp Hope, Houston, Texas.)

ACTIVITY 6

Speak Out

Audience: Youth.

Focus: To gather information and opinions about how youth view their community.

You will need: Index cards printed with four different questions (one question per card) and pencils for each participant.

Before the group arrives: Depending upon the size of the group you'll survey, the activity can take place with youth seated in groups on the floor or at tables. Each group should have four youth.

Set the stage: Explain to youth that their opinion matters, and the community would like to know what it can do to improve the atmosphere for young people. Youth will interview each other to answer a series of questions about the community. Each youth will receive an index card printed with one question. By the end of the activity, he or she will have recorded three responses to that question on the back of the index card. Questions can address whatever the community needs to know from youth. For example:

1. What makes our community special? What are we doing well?
2. What is wrong with our community? What don't we do well?

3. What do we need to do, add, or improve to make a difference in our community?

4. What are the top three challenges facing youth today?

Step 1: Distribute four cards (with four different questions) to each group of four students.

Step 2: For five minutes, students with questions 1 and 2 will interview each other and write responses, while students with questions 3 and 4 interview each other and write responses. After five minutes, ask students to switch partners, again ask each other questions, and record answers on the back. Call "time" at five minutes and ask them to switch partners one last time, repeating the interview with the remaining partners.

Step 3: Collect the answers, thank youth for participating, and share answers with the whole group. Later, compile the responses on a handout for use in future civic decision making.

Reflection Questions for Youth:

- Which questions had you not considered before?
- Which questions drew responses that you think adults most need to hear?

Reflection Questions for Adults:

- Which responses do you find the most surprising? Which responses make you feel proud? Nervous?
- Which youth responses do you feel provide the most crucial information?
- How should the group prioritize its efforts?

(Activity adapted with permission from Every Kid in Our Communities, Leeds and Grenville, Ontario, Canada.)

Moving from "Me" to "We"

- Write newspaper articles that educate community members about the great things youth are doing.

- Teach key people in power the value of youth perspective.

- Encourage city officials to utilize youth in making major decisions for the city.

- Be intentional about engaging young people in your daily activities.

- Seek funding to support youth empowerment opportunities.

- Smile at and greet youth; model the conversations adults can have with youth.

- Ask youth their opinions, and get behind their ideas.
- Invite friends and neighbors to attend a school function or athletic event.
- Invite youth to serve in leadership roles on traditionally adult decision-making committees.
- Start conversations with other adults about the great things you see youth accomplishing in the community.
- Stop at lemonade stands (and bake sales, car washes, and other youth-staffed endeavors)!

Did You Know?

At the Table, an initiative of the Innovation Center for Community and Youth Development (www.atthetable.org), is part of a growing national movement of youth and adults working to secure a place for youth "at the table" where decisions that affect them are made. Its Web site connects individuals, organizations, and communities to the resources they need to successfully involve youth in decision-making processes. It also provides networking opportunities for like-minded youth and adults, and gathers and shares stories from across the United States. At the Table publishes an online survey project that gathers opinions and data regarding service-learning, youth participation, voting age, youth school board membership, and other key issues affecting youth.

2

TREATING YOUTH AS VALUED RESOURCES

*"When our group was deciding what to name itself, Donna
Gillen said, 'Wait a minute. Let's ask the young people sitting
at this table.' The result was that [the group] was named
Alliance with Youth, rather than Alliance for Youth."*

—REBECCA JARVIS, CNBC TELEVISION BUSINESS CORRESPONDENT

Rebecca Jarvis has worked successfully in network journalism, invest-ment banking, and foreign currency trading. (She also earned the runner-up spot on the reality TV show *The Apprentice 4* in 2005.) Not surprisingly, Jarvis began her professional path as an empow-ered youth. She credits her parents with being the first to support her endeavors and treating her as an equal. Other key adults made a last-ing impact on her development as well. By age 15, Jarvis was show-ing the colors that would earn her the title of one of *Teen People's* "20 Teens Who Will Change the World."

As a teen representative of the Minnesota Youth Advisory Council, Jarvis helped advise the state legislature and represented her state as a delegate to the Presidential Summit in 1997. She also was a reporter for the Youth Advisory Council's Web site.

"I remember thinking [the summit] was a huge event—all the living presidents [were there, as well as] more than 3,000 people. But there were very few young people—only about 100," she says. "I remember the discontent among youth. The whole idea of the Presidential Summit was to bring people together to make a difference for young people, but the youth who attended had the feeling people thought youth were more a part of the problem than the solution."

She interviewed youth, celebrities, and General Colin Powell, whom Jarvis greatly respected. Jarvis says she told herself, "I could choose not to go up and talk to him, and then regret it, or I could see what would happen if I tried to get an interview."

So she approached Powell and inquired, "You want to help young people, but I see very few young people here. How do you expect to involve youth [so they] become a part of the solution?" Powell replied, "You have to take it back to your communities."

This was a turning point for Jarvis. She returned home and helped form what became the Minnesota Alliance with Youth, a nonprofit charity designed to integrate young people into leadership roles in all aspects of the community.

Building a Foundation: The Process Is Key

"Adults have to trust that youth are capable young leaders. We can do it all with them, not for them."
—DONNA GILLEN, EXECUTIVE DIRECTOR OF MINNESOTA-BASED YOUTHRIVE

The essential ingredient in any initiative that legitimately utilizes youth as resources is that it is youth-driven in some way. And organizations that serve young people must involve them in every step of the process, embracing the notion that youth have valuable ideas adults may never have considered.

In Lake Forest, Illinois, the Committee Representing Our Young Adults (CROYA) was established in 1980 as a youth agency run by youth, for youth, in response to problems teens were facing. The organization offers programs in youth leadership and life skills, community service projects, youth retreats and weekly gatherings, social

In 2003, cumulative data from the Search Institute Profiles of Student Life: Attitudes and Behaviors *survey revealed that only 26 percent of youth report they are given useful roles in their community. Take a moment to ask yourself how your community or organization stacks up as a place that promotes youth as valuable resources.*

Adult Inventory

In my community:

ALWAYS SOMETIMES NEVER

- ☐ ☐ ☐ Adults know how to step back without tuning out, and they encourage youth to build on their strengths.
- ☐ ☐ ☐ Adults listen to youth, challenge them to be good citizens, and look for ways to integrate their interests and strengths.
- ☐ ☐ ☐ Adults do not assume they know what youth are thinking; they ask them to share their opinions appropriately.
- ☐ ☐ ☐ Adults make time for youth decision making and input, recognizing the reciprocity of leading and learning.
- ☐ ☐ ☐ Adults partner with youth, creatively adapting adult roles to changing situations.
- ☐ ☐ ☐ Youth engage in research and evaluation efforts, and serve on the board of directors for youth organizations.
- ☐ ☐ ☐ Adults create formal and well-defined decision-making roles for youth, and provide leadership development resources.
- ☐ ☐ ☐ Organizations offer stipends and/or hourly pay for youth in leadership positions to help with recruitment and retention.
- ☐ ☐ ☐ Organizations offer a variety of leadership roles for youth throughout all aspects of their operations.
- ☐ ☐ ☐ Communities work toward broad and inclusive participation of hard-to-reach youth.
- ☐ ☐ ☐ Youth activism is seen as an important part of social movements fighting for democracy and justice.

Reprinted with permission from *Empowering Youth: How to Encourage Young Leaders to Do Great Things*, by Kelly Curtis, M.S. Copyright © 2008 by Search Institute, Minneapolis, Minnesota, 800-888-7828, www.search-institute.org. All rights reserved.

AN ENVIRONMENT RIPE FOR YOUTH EMPOWERMENT—WHAT YOUTH SAY

Take a moment to ask yourself how your community, school, or organization stacks up as a place that promotes youth as valuable resources.

Youth Inventory

In my community:

ALWAYS   SOMETIMES   NEVER

☐ ☐ ☐   Adults help me reach my goals; they're here for me, but they give me my space.

☐ ☐ ☐   Adults listen to me, challenge me to be a good citizen, and look for ways to tap into my interests and strengths.

☐ ☐ ☐   Adults ask me to share my opinion.

☐ ☐ ☐   Adults include youth in decisions and ask for input.

☐ ☐ ☐   Adults partner with young people on projects and change their role based on the situation.

☐ ☐ ☐   Youth serve on the board of directors for youth organizations, and help with research and evaluation.

☐ ☐ ☐   Young people understand the decision-making roles they're asked to fill; adults provide opportunities for youth to learn about leadership.

☐ ☐ ☐   Organizations offer stipends and/or hourly pay for youth in leadership positions to help with recruitment and retention.

☐ ☐ ☐   Organizations offer a variety of leadership roles for youth throughout all aspects of their operations.

☐ ☐ ☐   Communities ask all kinds of youth to participate in programs, including young people who might not seek out the opportunity.

☐ ☐ ☐   Youth activism is seen as an important part of social movements fighting for democracy and justice.

Reprinted with permission from *Empowering Youth: How to Encourage Young Leaders to Do Great Things,* by Kelly Curtis, M.S. Copyright © 2008 by Search Institute, Minneapolis, Minnesota, 800-888-7828, www.search-institute.org. All rights reserved.

activities, and peer support to youth in grades 7 through 12. Following its mantra, "start with youth," the organization defers to youth guidance in all matters.

Author Elaine Doremus Slayton, writing about CROYA in her book *Empowering Teens*, says that communities often create new activities and programs when trying to reach youth. But, she explains, "In their zeal and haste to do something, well-intentioned adults fail to recognize the most critical element—that any successful programming for youth must be youth-centered for it to work." Slayton describes what became known as the "CROYA Process":[1]

1. Youth or community suggests an idea.

2. Staff members listen and provide a larger forum of youth to discuss, and a youth committee votes to proceed with the idea.

3. A subcommittee of youth volunteers generates an extensive list of what the project entails.

4. The project is broken down into tasks, and individuals take responsibility, while staff members attend all meetings, facilitate the process, play "devil's advocate," and sustain the momentum.

5. A timetable is set, and youth complete assigned duties for each meeting, while staff work closely with committee chairs to ensure youth are on schedule.

6. On the day of the event, youth run the entire program, with help from staff; they arrive early and stay late.

7. All players complete written evaluations and discuss the outcome.

When adults talk about putting youth in charge, this is the point in the conversation where naysayers begin to squirm, wrinkle their brows, and explain all the reasons why it's not a good plan. Let's face it—we're uncomfortable giving up control and dealing with unknown quantities.

It's not that these concerns aren't valid. We face many challenges when we delegate responsibility to youth. Some responsibilities fall through the cracks. We ask for youth volunteers and are met with resistance or blank stares. But mistakes present an opportunity for learning, and all organizations experience growth as members learn the method of operations. The real question is, "What is the point of our group?"

If the mission of the organization is to prevent hazardous waste from seeping into groundwater, then it would not be appropriate for that organization to be led by young people. If the purpose of the initiative is to retrieve a military submarine from the crushing depths of the Pacific, then that's a job for adults as well. But if your organization has any connection with youth at all; if your policies impact the community, families, schools, or youth in general, there aren't many good reasons not to include youth in the decision making.

If adults have never witnessed youth leaders in action, they may simply not know it's possible. And individual attitudes can pose critical barriers to a person's ability to recognize youth as resources. Adults may need opportunities to learn about youth in order to truly understand their valuable perspective. When we see youth in action within the context of positive youth development, we're more likely to view youth as valued resources.

Don MacIntyre, principal of McNicoll Park Middle School, Penticton, British Columbia, Canada, makes a forceful point when he asserts, "Whether or not you choose to work to support young people, you will be the [beneficiary] of their decisions as they begin to assume leadership roles in society. I want them to be competent in those roles, because when it is time for my circle of influence to begin to diminish, I want to feel comfortable that I have left them in better shape than I have left their planet."

Initially, boards and committees include youth in order to benefit *youth*. Adults are hesitant to recognize that youth insights are equally as beneficial to their organization or community. But taking baby steps toward youth empowerment supports an organization's natural progression toward youth inclusion. Youth have the opportunity to become a genuine resource to adults, and over time, growth that occurs within members and policy makes youth inclusion possible.

Cindy Carlson, director of the Coalition for Youth in Hampton, Virginia, points out that "it's important for adults to understand where they really and honestly are in terms of believing that young people can be resources. That's the first step. And youth need to have a resource mentality, rather than a recipient or object mentality."

Mary Patterson, executive director of Project Cornerstone in San Jose, California, facilitates school workshops to help educators learn to view youth as resources, framed within the context of improving school climate. One teacher liaison and 10–15 youth identify trouble spots at school and create their own action plan. This same adult liaison helps them carry out their action plan in the school. Patterson says, "When youth are respected, they're going to feel they have a more caring climate."

Youth learn leadership by being leaders. Although mock leadership situations may effectively teach basic skills, youth need real-life opportunities to address genuine needs. If they aren't allowed to lead on their own, young leaders will lose interest. And in the most genuine youth development experiences, where youth are truly viewed as resources, both youth and adults learn. Adults open themselves to the possibility that they can experience personal growth as well.

Patricia Howell-Blackmore, director of communications and programs for Thrive! The Canadian Centre for Positive Youth Development, describes the accidental "aha" moment she experienced when she solicited silent auction donations from local merchants for a school fund-raiser. As she approached business owners, she says, "I was met with many polite smiles, but few were eager to donate."

Later in the week, she stopped to visit a local business with her daughter Hope, who is in grade 4. During Howell-Blackmore's fund-raising pitch, Hope mentioned that the funds generated the prior year purchased excellent new computer equipment for the library. Hope's sincere gratitude impressed the business owner and he made a generous donation to the event. Howell-Blackmore says:

> As we got back in the car, it dawned on me: Why shouldn't she be directly involved in the process behind the scenes? What better way to teach her about social responsibility? If kids know what goes on to make extra equipment available, it makes sense they will appreciate it more and take ownership for it. Now I'm scheduling our visits when Hope can come along. She does most of the talking, and I stand back, act as a support, and smile.

Changing Perspective–Letting Go

"If I have a set of standards, that's my perception of what is perfect. But what really makes it perfect?
- *That youth are totally engaged?*
- *That youth are experiencing the joy of the activity?*
- *That they are able to extend themselves to others?*
- *That they're able to communicate their wishes and desires?*
- *That youth bring their own voice and ideas?*
- *[Or is it] that they mirror the adult they want to please?"*

—MARILYN PEPLAU, TRAINER, SEARCH INSTITUTE VISION TRAINING ASSOCIATES

Marilyn Peplau, Vision Training Associates trainer and former school counselor, advised a group of Student-to-Student (STS) Peer Helpers at New Richmond High School in New Richmond, Wisconsin. In the early years of programming, adult advisors set and facilitated agendas for the training sessions. At one point, the students told Peplau, "We want this *not* to be like school at all. We'd like to lead it. How do we go about doing that?"

"This was a pivotal moment in the early years of STS," she says. "It was [about] guiding from behind—stepping back, so they could step forward." Sharing leadership and vision is not a simple task, because adults have to be able to relinquish some control. But Peplau says, "By redefining perfection, kids will exceed your expectations. They may go a different way than you would have, but it may be better than you could have planned it anyway."

Paula Gretzlock, peer tutoring advisor for Supportive Peers as Resources for Knowledge (SPARK) at New Richmond High School, knows how nerve-racking it can be to let go of the reins. "I fundamentally know that it's going to be fine, but it's hard to let go of that control. You have to be very trusting of youth. You need an idea of the end result, and even what you think key pieces will be. But you have to be vague enough that the kids don't think it's predetermined, or they'll limit themselves."

Gretzlock suggests offering youth a framework and an end goal, but letting youth determine the plan to get there. When youth create the plan, an advisor can ask them for solutions to any potential glitches in the plan near the end of the planning process.

"When they have an idea, let them go! They will think of 99 percent of the vital pieces. Their timeline might differ from yours a little bit, but they will do it," she says. "The coolest thing is afterwards they are so proud of themselves. It's the validation."

Organizational dynamics play a key role in the effectiveness of empowerment strategies. When Reservoir High School in Maryland opened its doors in 2002, only grades 9 and 10 were initially educated there, so they took on leadership roles traditionally held by grades 11 and 12. Principal Adrianne Kaufman, Ed.D., says, "Students who are empowered talk about the school in a positive way, and they don't just bring complaints to the administration, because they know to come with solutions as well."

Kaufman makes several suggestions for utilizing youth as resources in a school setting:

- Offer opportunities for youth to take on leadership roles and responsibilities.

- Invite teens to implement a principal's advisory program or conduct focus groups.

- Ask students to participate on the school improvement team and on staff committees.

- Send students to student leadership conferences.

- Ask students to lead asset-building activities through a school advisory program—typically during a homeroom period when youth meet with their homeroom teacher.

- Ask youth to evaluate new school programs and gather their suggestions for future programs.

- Maintain an "open door" policy in the principal's office so students know they're always welcome.

Growing Pains–After the "Letting Go"

"When I am handed responsibility, I feel as if people trust me.
I may make a mistake, but in the end, I feel I made a difference.
If an adult trusts a young person, the youth is most likely to treat
that responsibility with care and pride and grow as a person."

—CHRISTINE VIDMAR, RESERVOIR HIGH SCHOOL PROJECT COMMUNITY
GRADUATE AND PRINCETON UNIVERSITY STUDENT

Organizations that are new to the idea of letting go of the reins and giving up some of their power to youth members will undoubtedly experience growing pains. Adults tend to picture a project that differs from the vision youth have, and often try to orchestrate the process to fit their own vision, rather than opening their minds to the vision of youth.

Elaine Doremus Slayton, author of *Empowering Teens,* writes about the way community attitudes sometimes present obstacles to the success of a youth-adult partnership. CROYA youth agency approved the sponsorship of a concert in the Illinois suburbs after CROYA youth presented a thorough and impressive proposal for the production of the concert. Youth had worked diligently in collaboration with CROYA adults and the city manager to brainstorm concert logistics, potential complications, and solutions. They'd also recruited parent volunteers to chaperone the event. Their hard work and thoughtfulness convinced the agency to sponsor the project, and the city manager let them use the field outside the recreation center. Unfortunately, the concert was canceled because of rain. Oddly enough, neighbors called the police to complain about concert noise—*even though there wasn't any.*

Although youth knew they initially faced major community resistance to their concert plans, they pursued the project again the following summer. Because CROYA youth had gained the trust of city officials and CROYA adult board members throughout the planning of both projects, the following summer's concert occurred without incident and was a huge success.[2]

Sometimes simple logistics, like transportation, make it difficult to involve young people as resources in the community. Teens who live far from the center of school activity may not have readily available rides, which limits their extracurricular participation. Youth who have a car (or whose parents will drive them) or who live near public transportation are more likely to become involved.

Rebecca Jarvis remembers how critical it was that her mentor, Donna Gillen, took care of these logistics for members of the Minnesota Alliance with Youth:

> Donna picked us up in her car. She got cell phones and pagers [for all of us] so we could stay connected. She staged meetings at 8 P.M. because that's when it worked for us. She gave up many of the pleasantries of adult life to embody the spirit of youth.

CHALLENGES TO MEANINGFUL YOUTH INVOLVEMENT

Does your organization face these common challenges in trying to involve young people in meaningful ways?

- Meshing youth's school schedules with adult work schedules;
- Overcoming logistical barriers involving transportation and communication;
- Maintaining youth interest and commitment;
- Sharing power with young people;
- Viewing youth only as recipients of your organization, rather than as valued resources;
- Learning reciprocally between youth and adults; and
- Believing youth involvement will make a difference.

Effective Youth Empowerment Starts at the Beginning

Advisors of youth-centered programs often take on the full burden of coordinating positive youth development efforts. This can ultimately lead to burnout in even the most dedicated and outstanding asset builders. However, if adults can invest their efforts in empowering youth at the *outset* of a program, it will pay off in dividends for years. And the program will be more likely to sustain itself, gaining a life and momentum of its own.

Try these ideas to utilize youth as resources and reduce your load:

1. Recruit younger youth to learn from older participants, generating a cycle of trained replacements.

2. Initiate only projects that empower youth.

3. Keep an "idea board" for youth-generated suggestions. When it's time to address projects, you won't need to prepare a list.

4. Facilitate meetings—but don't lead them. Consider appointing a youth for this role, in an elected or rotating position.

5. Clarify your role. Are you a resource person? A periodic liaison? A token adult? This will eliminate any confusion over the group's expectations for you.

6. As an idea unfolds, create youth roles to fill needs—recorder, grant writer, permission getter, facility searcher, pizza supplier, sender of invitations, and so on.

7. Remember, empowerment is something youth want, and if they want it badly enough, they'll do what's necessary to make it happen. Guide youth through the steps, but don't take more ownership than they do.

ACTIVITY 7

Matchmakers

Audience: School staff.

Focus: To learn how to recognize and find opportunities for a range of youth leaders to be resources in the school.

You will need: Slips of paper for every staff member, whiteboard or overhead projector.

Set the stage: Young people can provide leadership in many ways, for a variety of school activities. Not all leaders are the assertive ones with excellent communication skills. This activity is an exercise in brainstorming names of all types of youth leaders—traditional, social, academic, quiet, athletic, and even "street" leaders.

Step 1: Ask teachers to write the names of all sorts of youth leaders on slips of paper, and ask them to note the ways in which they see the students as leaders.

Step 2: As the names are being collected, list the names, along with their leadership strengths, on a whiteboard or overhead transparency. Ask teachers to identify the leadership roles that youth on the list already fill. Then consider what other leadership opportunities exist that might be a good fit for youth leaders who have no identified roles.

Step 3: Ask teachers to volunteer to invite those youth to participate in the brainstormed leadership opportunities.

Reflection Questions:

- During the process of brainstorming youth leaders, were there names that surprised you?
- What new ways have you discovered to utilize youth leaders in your daily functions?
- What are some possible results from engaging youth in leadership roles within the school?

ACTIVITY 8

Project Plan

Audience: Youth.

Focus: To experience the planning process necessary to coordinate a youth initiative or project.

You will need: Chart paper, markers, tables that seat groups of four to six, large whiteboard.

Before the activity: This activity can be integrated into the agenda of any group that is learning about social change, service, civic action, or community improvement. Ideally, youth would have generated ideas already about an action they would like to pursue in the community or organization. If not, the group should discuss and decide upon a youth initiative or project they would like to coordinate. Create a transparency that lists the basic questions you need the group to answer, such as:

- Who is the audience for our project?
- Who are the stakeholders (or those who have an investment in this project)?

- What are the necessary resources?
- Which adults must be invited into the process?
- What are the considerations regarding the timing of the project or event?
- What are possible roadblocks or challenges?

Set the stage: Youth are talented members of the community, capable of accomplishing great things for the good of themselves and others. But without proper planning, initiatives can fail even for adults. This activity will guide youth through the planning process of their chosen project so that it has a greater likelihood of success.

Step 1: With the large group, share your transparency with basic questions that need to be addressed. Ask youth if there are other questions or concerns that should be added to the list. Organize the questions into sections so that they can be divided relatively evenly among the teams. Ask youth teams to choose the section of questions their team would like to address.

Step 2: Youth write each question on a separate piece of chart paper, and brainstorm answers to them. Remind teams to consider potential roadblocks and challenges, as well as ways to compensate for the challenges. After fully addressing a question, teams should generate a "to do" list of responsibilities necessary to answer concerns. Youth must be as specific as possible in their lists, including details such as the number of volunteers needed for each action item, commitment, and amount of time required, and approximate cost of the materials.

Step 3: After teams have addressed each question, they can post and share their planning sheets with the larger group. As a whole group, roles should be identified to manage the responsibilities listed for each topic. Youth choose a name for each role, and highlight its responsibilities. Ask for nominations and/or volunteers to fill each role, and adjust the workload as necessary. Most roles will be best accomplished in pairs or teams.

Step 4: Determine the first objectives and the date by which they are to be accomplished by each person, pair, or team.

Reflection Questions:

- How do you feel about what this group accomplished today?
- What group strategies were most effective today? Least effective?
- What could we do differently during our next meeting to meet our goals?

(Activity adapted with permission from Project Cornerstone, Santa Clara County, California.)

If Youth Are Our Future, We Need to Stop Procrastinating!

"Children are not 'citizens' in the making, but, instead, social agents who already participate in building strong and democratic communities."

—SILVIA BLITZER GOLOMBEK, PH.D., VICE PRESIDENT OF PROGRAMS, YOUTH SERVICE AMERICA

We often hear rhetoric about youth being the "leaders of tomorrow." While this sounds good, the message systematically promulgates the idea that youth are just "practicing"—that their input is really meaningless right now. Somehow, we imagine that as soon as they turn into grown-ups, they'll miraculously become people we should listen to. We don't seem to have a problem understanding that youth leadership opportunities help youth—with their self-esteem, confidence, and social competencies. But youth can positively impact the community as well, now and in the future. Many adults struggle to see youth leadership experiences as anything more than positive youth development.

Seeing is believing. Adults who witness empowered youth in action—or hold their breath and let go of the reins—can't deny the power in the experience. Ashley Pratte, 17, of Manchester, New Hampshire, joined the Manchester Mayor's Youth Advisory Council (MYAC) to affect policy and ensure that city government heard the voice of youth. As chair of the council, Ashley decided one way to promote civic engagement among young people was for the council to sponsor its own debates for state candidates running in the 2006 election. She played a lead role in organizing youth-run debates among the candidates for the state senate and executive council, and worked closely with the rest of the council to formulate questions and rules for the televised debates.

Pratte, a Prudential Spirit of Community Award state honoree, says:

My advisor for MYAC helped me to find my own direction. He helped to develop my confidence and to push me forward. He saw my passion for politics and community service, and he encouraged me to get involved in

other programs and activities. I know that Marty is someone that I can talk
to and go to for guidance because he treats me as though I were his equal
and not just a kid.

If we change the way we view youth, we change the way we utilize youth. And as more and more individuals in a community shift
their thinking, a new perception emerges—one that views youth as
resources and full-fledged citizens. It's a self-fulfilling prophecy. But
someone has to start the process.

Sometimes youth *want* to participate more than they're *prepared* to
participate. Training bridges the gap. A fine line floats between actively
engaging youth at their experience level and overwhelming them with
too much responsibility. And youth will fail if they have only artificial
status and no real power, or if they're burdened by responsibility that
has no connection to their former experience.

Cathann Kress, director of youth development for National 4-H
Headquarters, says that handing over complete power and responsibility to youth without first preparing them is "often nothing more than
abandonment by adults who are unsure how to partner effectively with
young leaders." Youth involvement can take time to grow into healthy
engagement. All parties need time and training to learn how to make
the partnership successful.[3]

Just as youth need preparation, so do adults. Whatever the group,
youth on a team deserve the same respectful communication as adult
team members. A simple reminder to all parties—whether it's about
using "I" statements or exhibiting appropriate manners—can foster
positive communication between youth and adults.

Groups can also employ strategies in their discussion process
that aid communication. Committees encourage participation by all
if they divide into smaller groups or follow rules during brainstorming sessions. Also, facilitators can ask questions that educate youth
through the process. Rather than pointing out that a suggestion isn't
reasonable, you can respectfully ask a question that pertains to your
roadblock: "How will we _____?" In this way, youth often discover for
themselves the avenues that best meet the demands of the project
without feeling they've been silenced.

Youth development researcher Carole MacNeil points out that the
modern trend in leadership styles is a move away from the concept of

leadership that resides in one person and toward the idea that leadership exists in the relationship between and among individuals—interdependent partnerships. This definition values shared power and collective action, which is ideal for youth participation. It also makes the process critically important. The ultimate partnership acknowledges that youth and adults each learn from each other, and that the experience would be much less valuable without the intergenerational dynamic.[4]

For instance, adults have the benefit of life experience and a sense of which projects are more likely to be successful. On the other hand, young people know what's meaningful to them and what will make an impact and inspire them.

Consider a screen door. As you look out the door, you see a barrier of tightly woven wire. But if you imagine yourself as a tiny mosquito, even the most insignificant tear in the mesh can serve as a huge portal into the comforts of home. Which do you see, the screen or the hole?

As we grow older, we gain valuable information about the world. Each piece of learning is woven into the "screen," adding to the realistic, overall picture of what can and cannot happen. It's vital that our society has people who see the screen. But likewise, we also need those who see the holes, the possibilities: those who don't become sidetracked by why something won't work. These idealists are often the catalysts for change.

The inexperience of youth sometimes makes it more possible to recognize what *can* happen rather than what cannot. It is the empowered young person who can use this unique ability to make a positive impact on the community. And it is the wise adult who listens to this perspective and works together with youth to discover a possible solution to a problem.

Some ideas generated by youth may seem unreasonable, but your patience can pay off in the long term. Several potential outcomes can result from a "crazy idea" that is allowed to go through the idea generation process without being stifled by adults:

- Youth will discover their idea is not a reasonable plan, and they'll drop the idea for a more realistic activity.

- Youth will pursue the crazy idea, it will flop, and afterward they'll process the mistake and learn from it.

- The crazy idea becomes a raving success, and critical adults are proved wrong!

The Freedom Writers, the "unteachable" first-year high school students of Long Beach, California, teacher Erin Gruwell, suggested to Gruwell that they organize a transatlantic visit from their classroom's heroine, Zlata Filipović, the young author of *Zlata's Diary: A Child's Life in Sarajevo*. In an attempt to squelch the idea with her adult-framed reality, Gruwell told her students, "If you want her to come, then you will have to raise the money to get her here." And within months, they'd done it![5]

Make Youth Authentic Participants

"As adults we sometimes think we know what the kids want and offer programs accordingly. Often, what we think is going to be a sure success only meets with failure, as evidenced by a lack of participation and a 'that is so lame' opinion from the kids. If we can't get kids to participate, we are wasting our time and our resources."

—MARYLEE BLACKWELL, OLD SAYBROOK, CONNECTICUT

We know youth leadership development positively impacts youth participants, but it can also benefit society as a whole. Organizations become more effective and relevant by shifting their thinking and practice to recognize youth for what they have to offer, rather than just for what they need.

Each year, youth from high schools throughout Charlotte County, New Brunswick, Canada, take turns in coordinating and planning a youth rally for 100 young people. They work with a budget, raise funds, emcee the event, and organize the registration process. Youth work with hotel staff to coordinate rooms, menus, and contracts. They also hire keynote speakers and facilitate learning sessions. Eleven St. Stephen High School students organized the very first conference, which they called "Shake Your Assets." They managed a $5,000 budget to coordinate a conference that would educate youth about Search Institute's survey results and asset development.

MAKING MEETINGS GO SMOOTHLY

Be sure to take into consideration the following logistics to ensure successful meetings with youth:

- Establish appropriate boundaries regarding policies and procedures for all group members—the bylaws, traditions, and underlying assumptions about who gets to vote—prior to inviting youth to participate.

- Communicate clearly with all participants and be consistent in following up with answers to questions and concerns youth may have about transportation, agenda, and their role in the process.

- Be aware of conflicts youth and adults may have with meeting times. Youth are as busy as adults and are more likely to participate in joint projects if you're sensitive to their schedules.

- Meet in easily accessible, youth-friendly locations like community centers, YMCAs, and pool halls.

- Innovate ways to keep youth connected to issues and discussions.

Project leader Chandra Leavitt says:

Adults learned that youth are capable of much more than we give them credit for and will always step up to the challenge if given the chance. They also learned that special communication skills are necessary in engaging youth. It is necessary to guide them and ensure [their] boundaries are respected, while at the same time knowing that it is [important] not to dictate adult desires.

The most successful organizations create "scaffolding" or a structure that engages youth along the way in a variety of leadership positions—in planning, evaluating, and decision-making roles. And the ways youth are involved in the decision making can vary to fit the needs of the organization—or the youth. Young people can participate in large and small ways, and it's this variety that makes it possible to engage youth in all forms of decision making.

It may be inappropriate to use the terms "youth leadership" and "youth development" interchangeably. Some youth truly have the skills, talent, and character to be exceptional leaders, and they deserve opportunities that offer unique experiences designed for aspiring leaders. However, expecting all youth to funnel through the same leadership experience will result in mediocre experiences for all.

Youth leadership can be integrated into a variety of programs, settings, and initiatives in which youth with diverse talents and skills can participate. The Young Women's Leadership Alliance of Santa Cruz, California, promotes a range of leadership styles and roles—timekeeper, "vibes watcher," and scribe—allowing all girls to be leaders with defined roles, even those who don't feel comfortable facilitating a group.[6]

The beauty of viewing youth as valued resources is that there are a variety of ways to do so. If communities and organizations make youth engagement a priority, they can always find an appropriate fit for youth and the project.

Youth as Board Members and Advisors

"They know the problems in the community and if we just work with them instead of squelching their ideas, they come up with brilliant and functional plans that can be executed. Adults need to embrace the fresh ideas of youth."

—PAULA MORRIS, FOUNDER AND PRESIDENT OF KIDS OF HONOR, INC.

Some communities incorporate youth into existing adult governing bodies—planning commissions, councils, and committees. Youth exercise an equal vote alongside adults, and voice their views about the direction of the organization. The youth empowerment organizations Youth on Board and At the Table offer resources and online networking to help communities engage youth in decisions that affect them.

Some say if youth have no vote, there's no point. Christine Vidmar, a student at Princeton University and graduate of Project CommUNITY, says:

> I worked with our county's board of education. We have a student member
> on the board, but [that person does] not have voting rights. Many adults in
> the community felt now was not the time and place for a student to [become

a voting member]. "How can they be making decisions about MY tax dol-
lars?" or "They're just children, they don't know enough to vote." These types
of comments from adult community members really infuriated me.

The youth cochair of the positive youth development organization Children First in St. Louis Park, Minnesota, plays an equal role
with the adult cochair in setting the direction, planning, and running
of meetings, as well as representing the initiative as a spokesperson.
Youth serve on many boards and commissions throughout the city
and school district.

The YMCA's national program, Youth in Government, works with
nonprofits, city governments, and tribal groups to facilitate youth
placement in decision-making roles on community boards and committees in Alaska. Daniel Gillespie, a former project participant, says:

By putting youth on the boards of these youth organizations, [the organiza-
tions] are better able to serve their constituents, and the youth involved feel
more valued and better able to direct the path of the organization.

But David Huether, volunteer for Every Kid in Our Communities,
in Leeds and Grenville, Ontario, Canada, suggests that youth inclusion
on adult committees may be an imperfect solution:

[Youth] are put in a difficult position—a board of trustees with two students
and 25 adults? That's an unfair situation for those young people. There's got
to be a way to get young people involved in a way that honors them rather
than making them the two token youth.

A growing number of youth organizations and agencies are incorporating young people into adjunct councils and task forces that report
to the larger governing body. The New Brunswick (Canada) Advisory
Council on Youth voices the interests, needs, concerns, and perspectives of young people ages 15 to 24, and presents their recommendations to local governments and to the public. The council gives youth a
vehicle to identify matters that concern them and encourages greater
youth integration into society. Since 2004, the council has sponsored
statewide youth conferences to recognize and promote community
involvement and civic engagement. The forums teach youth ways to
get involved every day to make a difference in New Brunswick.

The city of Santa Barbara, California, also taps into youth perspective. In 2003, youth council advisory members suggested that an empty building in Santa Barbara be converted into a teen center. Initially, the city council opposed the idea. Susan Young, supervisor of teen programs for the city of Santa Barbara, explains that three youth council advisory members came before the city council and said, "You have a youth council, but you don't use us as an advisory body." City council members asked them to return with a proposal, so the youth created a slide presentation, complete with diagrams and revenue potential for a teen center. Young says, "It was better than any other adult presentation the [council] had ever seen."

For three years, a revolving group of youth consistently came back to the council to remind members about the need for teen center funding, the importance of young people's involvement, and to push along the drawn-out process. Youth designed the floor plan, developed programs, wrote policies, determined logistics, and chose activities and colors. Youth participated in hiring a manager when interviewees came to a teen center meeting. Young says:

> One of the women was totally overwhelmed by them. She was expecting the youth conversation to be about "What kind of pizza [should we serve]?" She couldn't believe how they were totally in control of the meeting.

In March 2007, the teen center opened, a project entirely for youth, by youth.

The strongest model for youth inclusion may be a combination of ad hoc youth input, as well as formal board membership. Karen Young, of Youth on Board, advises using both a small number of youth positions on a governing board *and* a youth advisory committee that makes recommendations on key issues, representing the larger perspective.[7] Similarly, the Hampton Coalition for Youth utilizes an accordian-style process in which a group gathers, youth then meet together separately from adults, and then youth return to the larger intergenerational setting for dialogue.

Regarding Hard-to-Reach Youth as Valued Resources

"Youth leaders shouldn't be just the status quo kids who want to raise their hands and be on the honor roll. There are tons of other leaders who never raise their hands. It's important to look at every young person in terms of leadership potential. Youth can make decisions if given the proper scaffolding, support, tools, and education."

—MOLLY DELANO, YMCA NEW YORK CITY ASSET LAB PROJECT

Often, diversity is seen as a challenge to youth leadership. But groups that represent their constituency and embrace diversity are more likely to make decisions that matter, make sense, and are supported by constituents.[8] Successful youth organizations are sometimes elitist in terms of who has access to them, so programs must be attractive and relevant to target audiences with regard to income level, race, gender, ability, and ethnicity. We *must* find ways to connect with underrepresented and hard-to-reach youth, and support them through progressively more challenging leadership roles.

Prudential Spirit of Community Awards state honoree Morgan McDonald, 14, of Aurora, Colorado, helps lead a group in her school that works to build leadership skills and improve scholastic achievement among African American students. She meets with other group members every week to brainstorm ways to improve their education, challenge students to succeed in school, and change the way people look at students of color. Morgan helped raise funds to host a daylong community conference on the theme "Building Leadership in the African-American Community for Kids." She says:

> I feel like everyone needs to know that there is an achievement gap and that there are positive ways of solving it. At my school, we planned a conference to talk about it. It was a great event . . . Now that I have won this award, I am finding myself in special places doing things I never thought I'd be doing. I realize that working hard is important to have success.

Morgan advises adults who want to engage youth in their planning and projects to "look in different cultures for the abilities they have [to offer]. Don't always look for the same things in everyone. Everyone has something special to offer."

Socioeconomic factors sometimes pose the most significant barriers to youth inclusion. And without intentional practices in place, youth from low-income families will be least likely to be offered opportunities.

Wisconsin school principal Wayne Whitwam recalls growing up in poverty. Although his family was a loving and nurturing one, his parents rarely accepted social charity, and during a difficult period, Whitwam was homeless for two years. He recalls:

> I was the kid that claimed I didn't want the candy bar. I said I wasn't hungry for lunch. When the teacher told us each to bring $2.00 the next day for the pizza party, I just said I didn't like pizza. That's how you cope, so people don't know you're poor.

Whitwam instantly recognizes that coping mechanism in the youth at his school, and works hard to ensure youth receive the opportunities they've earned, regardless of cost. "Low-income kids are selected for opportunities, but if they believe there's a cost involved, they'll come up with an excuse for why they can't go. They won't say money is the issue—it will be something else. But people don't always see the signs. They need to know youth well enough to [see] through the mask."

Foster children are sometimes the most difficult to reach. But even for hard-to-reach youth, empowering them can be just giving them an avenue to do what they're already primed to do. At 13, Heather Wilder of Las Vegas, Nevada, wrote a series of booklets to help foster children understand and cope with their situations based on her own experiences as a foster child. She says:

> You don't always know what is going on or what to expect. I thought [that if they had] some books about issues that I faced, or that some other foster kids face, it would be an important thing to have when they travel from home to home.

Heather wrote the booklets with another former foster child, Raven Asay, and produced them with help from her new mother and a grant from the city of Las Vegas. The booklets are three to four pages long and are designed to address the challenges foster children face while preparing them for people and situations they may never have encountered previously: "Why do I have to move again? What is a social worker? What is this court talk all about?" To write the booklets, the girls would choose a title, brainstorm, type up the content, and draw a cover. What they needed from adults was financial and logistical support, which was provided by Heather's mom and the grant. Heather says she encourages adults to figure out what talents a young person has and "go all the way to help them build on it."

But not all populations are assertive enough to share their thoughts. The Young Women's Leadership Alliance found that girls struggle to articulate their thoughts and feelings in some settings, so advisors used assertiveness strategies that helped the girls to know and use their voices. The adults promoted a safe and trusting environment, and facilitated the group in making its own ground rules, with smaller group discussions to encourage participation from those who spoke less. The advisors identified and encouraged leadership styles and roles not associated with traditional definitions of leadership, and then facilitated a high-interest discussion (on topics such as justice and equality), expecting all girls to participate.

Alliance adult leaders also introduced a decision-making process based on coming to a group consensus that promoted a norm of respectful disagreement among *all* youth, not just those with assertive communication skills. It was designed as a place where girls could be authentic—where they could be themselves and be heard.

Youth as Change Agents

"If there are social or political things going wrong that need to change, you need to look to young people to make those changes. "

—MOLLY DELANO, YMCA NEW YORK CITY ASSET LAB PROJECT

The YMCA Asset Labs in New York City are community-based organizations in an area that has a greater than 50 percent high school dropout rate. Lab coaches empower many hard-to-reach youth while helping them examine the economic and social issues that present barriers in their lives. The 18 Asset Labs infuse the Developmental

Assets into everything they do and work in partnership with schools and community-based organizations.

"[The Asset Lab approach] is a democratic way of youth organizing. It's a sustainable youth empowerment vehicle. It's a lifelong thing. In organizations or as individuals, it's young people making their voices heard," explains Molly Delano.

In 2002, the City University of New York briefly raised the in-state tuition rates it charged undocumented immigrants to higher out-of-state rates in response to the Illegal Immigration Reform and Immigrant Responsibility Act of 1996, a federal law. One of the Asset Labs in New York took the lead in a campaign to fight for immigrant rights and repeal this law.

Delano says, "As an adult you have to be ready with insight to be able to support decisions the youth make. You'll be talking less and less. You can step back more and more." Eventually, New York governor George Pataki signed a state law restoring the lower in-state tuition rates for undocumented immigrants who met residency and diploma criteria.

Delano says youth organizing groups are often politically based, progressive, and committed to social justice and change. Sista II Sista is a Brooklyn-wide community-based organization of young adult, working-class, Black and Latina women. It works with young women to develop personal, spiritual, and collective power while fighting for justice and creating alternatives to the systems in which they live. For example, in 2003 Sista II Sista was part of a large coalition that fought to keep school program funding that was to be redirected to youth incarceration budgets. The initiative succeeded in achieving its goal.

Social change can also come from individual youth who recognize a need and do something about it. In New Richmond, Wisconsin, a small group of inspired young individuals addressed a politically charged issue in their conservative community. They saw the need for understanding and tolerance regarding their gay, lesbian, bisexual, and transgendered (GLBT) friends at school, and chose to address the issue by sponsoring a 10 Percent Society informational meeting. They invited members from a local chapter to lead a discussion and educate community members. It was a critical night, because these youth stepped into an advocacy role their GLBT friends could not assume socially, and school staff could not assume politically.

It's difficult to ignore the potential far-reaching, long-term, renewable, and permanent effects that can result from helping youth connect to their communities in ways that make social change. Perhaps the most critical way to spread the word about utilizing youth as resources is to let the world see you and other adults utilize youth as resources. Young people can be the best educators for how other adults can use youth strengths to better the community.

Relationships Are Key

"[Empowerment] was people who constantly said 'You can do that' and 'What do you think about this?' It's pushing you and challenging you and supporting you at the same time."

—RHONDA WILLERS, NEW RICHMOND (WISCONSIN) HIGH SCHOOL
GRADUATE AND STUDIO ARTIST

Viewing youth as resources is not a program or an initiative implemented by a committee. It's a choice we make to integrate a belief system into our daily lives. It's being the one who sees something in a young person that she doesn't even see herself.

Leslie Janca, coordinator for the Georgetown Project in Georgetown, Texas, says we can accomplish a lot by broadening and extending what we do in our homes to include the kids next door:

You're already doing this in your daily life to support your own kids. [If the] kids down the block . . . knew you were always there for them, it would make a big difference . . . You [don't have] to learn something new, but can build upon what you already do.

Rhonda Willers, New Richmond (Wisconsin) High School graduate, remembers being most intrigued by reflective adults who promoted broad thinking in young people:

They were opinionated. They had strong beliefs in their ideas, and perceived their philosophies with passion in their lives. They were optimistic or idealistic, because you have to be in order to pursue something passionately. Many don't have role models who are people that really believe in what they do.

We also need to acknowledge the power of youth culture. "Adults need to try to understand, or at least respect, our music preferences and our style of clothing," says Lisa Silverman, 17, a student at Centennial High School in Ellicott City, Maryland. We can make relationship inroads by understanding the language, the gestures, the celebrity icons, and fashion trends that matter to young people.

Molly Delano of the YMCA New York City Asset Lab Project comments, "Culture is key. Not just ethnic, or neighborhood, but artistic culture: music and song. It's so fundamental for a person who works with youth to be open to it." CROYA staff members in Lake Forest, Illinois, go out of their way to create a social environment for youth and to connect with youth at their own level—providing food, listening to popular music, and even dressing the part.

Of course, this wouldn't constitute an authentic interaction for every adult. Adults need to know the role they play and feel comfortable in it. Just having a genuine enthusiasm for and interest in youth can be equally effective. Daniel Gillespie, former Alaska Spirit of Youth participant, says of Becky Judd, an adult cofounder of Spirit of Youth:

> What sets Becky apart is that she can be an adolescent herself. She is able to be authoritative when necessary, but knows that sometimes kids just need to be let go for a while. She knows when to put the pressure on us to perform and when to back off because we're exhausted from school, too giggly to work, or anything in between. Whereas many adults, I think, take this kind of immaturity on our part as a reason to not empower us, Becky knows it is just part of our age and has nothing to do with our ability to achieve.

Whether you're the parent or the coach, the teacher or the mayor, when all is said and done, the relationship's the thing. Teenagers need guidance to grow into the leaders they are destined to become, and they're eager for the opportunity to volunteer. For us to truly envision youth as the resources they are, we must begin to utilize their capabilities, ask their opinions, recognize their input, and follow their lead.

ACTIVITY 9

Town Map

Audience: Adult and youth civic leaders.

Focus: Brainstorm ways to integrate youth into civic positions of influence and authority.

You will need: Room set up in table groups of six to eight, flipchart paper or overhead projector, and markers for each table. Invite youth to cofacilitate the activity.

Before the group arrives: Compile a broad list of community youth participation or leadership roles and be sure to invite people connected with these parts of the community. Write your list on a flipchart or overhead transparency. Consider minor and major roles to illustrate a range of opportunity.

Set the stage: Explain that most people understand that youth participation in civic activities positively impacts the youth, but that many don't recognize the ways the organizations and adults can benefit as well. Describe the ways that youth benefit the organizations in which they serve (see page 40). Introduce the activity by explaining ways youth participate and provide leadership in various communities. Discuss the list you compiled earlier. Be sure that each table group is composed of both youth and adult participants (preferably at least two of each).

Step 1: Ask each group to use their markers to draw a large outline map of their town on the chart paper. Participants should identify civic, educational, religious, service, and other community organizations, groups, or boards where they would be found on the map. Encourage participants to consider small and large roles, long-term and short-term commitments. Work toward a broad and comprehensive map.

Step 2: Allow the brainstorming process to continue as long as ideas flow. Next, on a separate sheet of chart paper, make a vertical line down the paper to create two columns. In one column, ask participants to list current opportunities for youth representation on governing bodies, and in the other column, list current opportunities for adjunct bodies. Then, with a different color marker, brainstorm ways the other organizations or groups on the map might be able to integrate youth into decision-making processes. Include youth representation opportunities currently available in the community in a different color.

Step 3: Ask each group to share its list with the larger group, and discuss which suggestions might be the first ones to pursue. Also discuss ways to promote the ideas in the community. Compile a final report to be shared with all participants, as well as organizations that were unable to attend.

Reflection Questions:
- How do you feel about the brainstormed list, as well as the mapped opportunities?

- How does or will youth involvement affect these community organizations?
- Which community locations could we prioritize for encouraging youth involvement?

Get Involved!

Audience: Youth.

Focus: To introduce young people to the council process and current community issues.

You will need: Access to a city council or other board meeting, the flexibility to transport or meet youth at a time when the meeting is in session.

Before the meeting: Ask the council for the minutes from the previous meeting so that you can discuss and learn about current issues prior to attending. Ask youth how they feel about the issue, with the information they have. What questions do they have about the issue? What do they hope to discover at the meeting?

Set the stage: Prepare youth for the expected behavior and dress at the meeting, the anticipated agenda, and at what time it might be appropriate to ask questions.

Step 1: Take youth to the council meeting. Model interactions with council members by greeting them before or after the meeting and introducing yourself and your students. Encourage youth to get acquainted with people who are making decisions.

Step 2: Afterward, ask the group to choose one issue they'd like to address. Research, write letters to council members, and talk to people about the issue. Then ask that youth be included on the agenda of a future meeting to voice their opinions about the issue.

Step 3: Attend a second council meeting so youth have an opportunity to voice their opinions.

Reflection Questions:

- What was the most important lesson you learned from this project?
- Are there issues you were introduced to here that you plan to become involved with in the future?
- Did you meet anyone during this process that you think you will meet again? How?

(Activity adapted with permission from Barbara Varenhorst, Ph.D.)

Moving from "Me" to "We"

- Encourage youth participation within organizations in which you serve a role.

- Create a youth-friendly environment in all aspects of your life.

- Encourage young people to speak up and share what's on their minds.

- Help youth to be resourceful—to find the answers to their questions.

- Model respectful communication. Other adults will learn by watching you.

- Invite youth to participate in—or lead—initiatives and presentations that would showcase their abilities in public.

- Defer to young people when others ask questions that would be answered most appropriately by youth.

- Help youth and adults make connections between social issues, between current and historical perspectives, between the local and global situation, and between their lives and those of others.

Did You Know?

Thirteen-year-old Prudential Spirit of Community Awards honoree Alexander Jonlin helped draft and pass a bill in the Washington State Legislature that created a 22-member youth advisory council to represent young people's perspectives on state legislative matters. Jonlin researched youth councils in other states, testified at hearings, and traveled around the state to lobby for the bill's passage. As a member of the new council, Alexander addresses issues important to young people, and is lobbying to pass another bill that would extend the youth council's term.

SERVING THE NEEDS
OF OTHERS

*"Young people wish to make a difference in the
world. And they can see they're making a difference
[when there's] someone to advocate for them."*

—DAVID HUETHER, COMMUNITY VOLUNTEER, EVERY KID
IN OUR COMMUNITIES OF LEEDS AND GRENVILLE, ONTARIO

Ryan Hreljac's grade 1 teacher told his class that children were dying
in the world because they didn't have access to the plentiful and clean
water enjoyed by Canadians. She said $70 would be what it took to
build a well. Ryan recalls:

> It just struck me. I counted the steps it took me to get to the water fountain
> outside my classroom, and I compared it to the thousands of steps that
> people in Africa had to take. I didn't think it was fair that children were
> getting sick and even dying because they didn't have clean water to drink.

Ryan went home and asked his parents for $70. "They told me I
couldn't have the money, but [suggested] I could do extra chores to
earn it," he says. For months, Ryan did extra chores, and when he
finally earned the $70, he discovered the well would actually cost
$2,000.

So Ryan did more chores.

With support from the nonprofit organizations WaterCan, Canadian Physicians for Aid and Relief, Canadian International Development Agency, and Free the Children, in less than a decade Ryan's fund-raising has grown to over $1,500,000. He says:

> I started with one well more than nine years ago, and now with so much support from others, we have built 266 wells in 12 developing countries that bring clean water and proper sanitation facilities to almost 450,000 people.

Ryan credits his mom and dad for supporting his dream since the very beginning. With their help, he founded the Ryan's Well Foundation and has delivered his "power of one" message to well over a million people through speaking engagements, talk show appearances, and hundreds of articles.

A combination of experiences helped Ryan believe he could make a difference—learning about this need in Africa, receiving encouragement from family and friends, having a strong moral foundation, and being given a chance to change people's lives. He says, "When I went to Uganda and saw how happy people were just because they had clean water, it made me even more determined to keep on helping."

His amazing story is not an isolated one. In fact, each year Prudential Financial honors youth for their exemplary acts of volunteerism with its Prudential Spirit of Community Awards. Prudential's 2007 report lists more than 300 service projects, including those of a young inventor who developed a method for removing harmful chemicals from neighborhood water sources and a Chinese American adoptee who raised money to create libraries in Chinese orphanages. Community service has certainly expanded beyond candy striping and litter pickups of years past.

In literature and practice, "volunteerism" is often used interchangeably with "service" and covers a wide range of opportunities, levels of commitment, and roles. No longer is community service just a school graduation or court requirement. Service projects can be "one-time only" events, long-term community partnerships, or one-to-one relationships sustained over time. Some service focuses on social and political learning and activism as well.

The arms of service are multiplying as youth find ways to bring to the table their own interests, aptitudes, strengths, and passions. Adding to our understanding of volunteerism are service-learning, service politics, youth philanthropy, and all the individual, group, short-term, long-term, leader, and participant roles within them.

Building a Foundation

"The likely result of instilling the service habit in children and youth will be significant long-term benefits—to young people, their families, schools, and communities—that our current research barely begins to capture."

—PETER SCALES AND EUGENE ROEHLKEPARTAIN IN *GROWING TO GREATNESS*

In *Growing to Greatness*, Search Institute researchers Peter Scales and Eugene Roehlkepartain refer to "service to others" as a "gateway" asset. Just as gateway drugs can lead youth to engage in risky behaviors and experience personally harmful outcomes, gateway assets can lead youth to more Developmental Assets and positive outcomes, because assets work together to provide a strong foundation for healthy development.[1]

The authors point out that service participation may both result from and contribute to a web of assets that, together, impact human development more significantly than can one asset alone. They call service an "authentic form of learning" because it connects to real-world needs, and may motivate the least engaged students in a way that a traditional curriculum cannot.

In the 1990s, youth volunteer rates increased by 12 percent across the United States. Surveys show that 83 percent of America's public high schools organize some form of community service for their students. And 73 percent of America's 60 million young people believe they can make a difference in their communities. But while some studies show that young people are participating in service activities at a rate higher than at any time in the past 50 years, only 48 percent of youth report serving in the community one or more hours per week. Search Institute encourages communities to elevate the importance of

HOW DOES YOUR COMMUNITY RATE?
Creating a Space That Encourages Youth to Value Service to Others

The following attitudes and behaviors characterize a community that places a high value on caring for its residents and providing service to those in need. Take a moment to ask yourself how your community is doing when it comes to providing youth with a strong foundation for service to others:

ALWAYS SOMETIMES NEVER

☐ ☐ ☐ Our service projects and initiatives use local and culturally relevant concepts and language.

☐ ☐ ☐ Our service projects integrate learning and reflection, including socio-historical contexts.

☐ ☐ ☐ Our initiatives use clear, conversational language for goals, definitions, and evaluation.

☐ ☐ ☐ Our community uses thoughtful planning and makes connections between short-term projects and long-term, comprehensive community development.

☐ ☐ ☐ Local foundations include youth decision makers in philanthropic infrastructure.

☐ ☐ ☐ Community service organizations create a youth-friendly atmosphere, engage youth as decision makers, and connect youth and adults as partners.

☐ ☐ ☐ Adults consistently consider ways to involve youth in active service leadership positions.

☐ ☐ ☐ Adults advocate for and prepare young people to interact as equals in a variety of service settings.

☐ ☐ ☐ Service organizations involve youth from diverse backgrounds to reflect the various constituencies in our community, and distribute leadership opportunities across youth populations.

☐ ☐ ☐ Youth service leaders do an excellent job of recruiting other youth participants.

☐ ☐ ☐ Our community expands and promotes service leadership roles for youth.

☐ ☐ ☐ Youth service organizations partner with community organizations to carry out successful projects.

Reprinted with permission from *Empowering Youth: How to Encourage Young Leaders to Do Great Things*, by Kelly Curtis, M.S. Copyright © 2008 by Search Institute, Minneapolis, Minnesota, 800-888-7828, www.search-institute.org. All rights reserved.

service and ensure that all youth engage in acts of service to their communities many times per year from the ages of 5 through 20.[2]

Youth give several reasons why they participate in service—they have compassion for people in need; they want to do something for a cause they believe in; they believe if they help others, others will help them; and it's a way to hang out with friends. And the benefit list is long. Youth volunteers:

- Are more likely to volunteer as adults;

- Learn to respect others, and become empathetic, patient, helpful, and kind;

- Develop leadership skills and good citizenship;

- Increase their political awareness and desire to become politically active;

- Understand sociohistorical contexts, politics, and morality in society, and how to effect social change;

- Experience higher academic achievement and social competence;

- Experience increased altruism, a sense of personal responsibility, and concern for others' welfare;

- Experience increased self-esteem and a sense that one can make a difference; and

- Experience improved parent-child relationships (Scales and Roehlke-partain, 2004).

Partnering for a Culture of Service

"It's teaching adults the ministry of stepping back—you lead, participate, teach, then step back—always stepping back,"

—PEGGY CONTOS-HAHN, ON THE QUALITIES NEEDED IN A CAMP HOPE ADULT MENTOR

Sometimes adults hesitate to become involved in service projects because they're afraid they'll become overwhelmed. But if initiatives structure service opportunities to foster youth and adult partnerships, then each person shares part of the responsibility and each volunteer benefits from the other's participation. As a by-product, adults who volunteer as partners with youth are more likely to see young people as positive contributors to the community. The endless list of ways to partner gives every adult and every youth the opportunity to participate in a way that's life-giving and fills a need.

Karen Atkinson, coordinator of Children First in St. Louis Park, Minnesota, helped her son's grade 4 classroom apply for and receive a $500 grant from Youth Service America (YSA). The children came up with the idea, researched it, interviewed people, conducted a survey, wrote the grant proposal, implemented the project, and sent a summary to YSA. They purchased audiotape books for the English Language Learners (ELL) class. Atkinson says:

> This [project] was an eye-opener to me. I work with lots of teenagers and know of their capabilities, but was surprised and impressed at what these 10-year-olds could grasp and do. Young people want to help others. Adults need to provide assistance when needed, but [should] not take over projects.

Atkinson encourages parent organizations to think about where young people can play a service role. She asks them, "Can older athletes help younger players through Little League? Can older students volunteer to work [with younger students in] booths at the school carnival?"

Julia Hampton, coordinator of the Windham County (Vermont) Youth Initiative, says this partnership is about more than just requiring student service hours for graduation. A school's community service requirement *does* demonstrate that the school values service and encourages youth to become participants in the community. But, she says, a service partnership between youth and adults is not just about the service. "If adults can be more intentional about walking alongside youth, [the service itself] will become more meaningful."

Service activities provide an opportunity for youth and adults to work together in solving community problems and improving quality of life. In the process of working toward common goals, youth and adults engage in meaningful dialogue and develop trust and respect for each other. Erik Laursen, past president of Strength-Based Services International, Virginia, writes that "the cultivation of positive peer relationships in school, sports teams, street corners, and community systems involves mobilizing youth as leaders in building positive peer cultures that focus on solving problems and helping one another."

Adult partners in service help young people discover their innate motivation to help others. The side-by-side interaction gives compassionate adults an opportunity to model a sense of responsibility and social conscience. The more often youth and adults participate in a project like this, the stronger the group becomes. Like-minded people working toward a common community goal—it's powerful stuff.

Camp Hope, a youth-led, adult-mentored, congregation-based summer day camp ministry in Houston, Texas, assists congregations with staffing and mentoring high school students who run a day camp in their neighborhood. The system prepares youth for future leadership roles. Starting in grade 5, campers take on increasingly more responsible positions in the camp program. Paid staffers also direct special projects with significant responsibilities, and the camp manager is a college student. Youth serve on the national team that trains congregations throughout the country to coordinate a Camp Hope program. In an effort to put young people on a direct path to leadership within their congregation, the training program requires teams of three youth and three adults to participate in the workshop.

Adult mentors provide the most critical element of the program. Each youth staff member partners with an adult mentor, beginning six weeks before the camp begins, and continuing one week after camp is over. "The hardest part is teaching adult mentors their role—they play a critical role, but not the one they're used to. They're not 'hands on' in the ministry. They're actually [working] behind the scenes," says Peggy Contos-Hahn, the founder of Camp Hope. "Sometimes a youth is overly confident, and crashes and burns—then the mentor needs to help that youth get up and go back [to work] the next day."

Religious organizations often take the lead in service projects within a community. Churches facilitate partnerships between adult congregation members and youth group participants. And members of all ages rally around global mission opportunities. The Children, Youth, and Family Ministry arm of the Lutheran Church of Australia in Adelaide, South Australia, cultivates caring youth and adult partnerships through local and overseas service projects, as well as offering opportunities for coaching, mentoring, and reflecting on best practices.

This Christian youth organization supports young people and adults who work with young people throughout South Australia and the Northern Territory, seeking to empower youth through participation in various programs and services. Adult staff are encouraged to take an interest in all young people who spend time in the building. Director Peter Eckermann says, "Our president [CEO] especially makes a point of finding out the names of young people and remembering them, and finding out what a particular young person is working on and what their passions are."

Eckermann says people and relationships make the projects successful. "You can hear the sound of young people, youthful enthusiasm, energy, vitality. You can hear the sound of the 'young at heart,' too, as they engage in conversation with young people. Youth are made to feel welcome, wanted, encouraged, and valued. The young at heart say that the thing they value most in the environment is the presence of young people and their amazing contributions."

The church offers service opportunities locally, such as "The Big Week Out," a weeklong program of youth-led community service, as well as overseas field experiences to places such as Cambodia. Organizers are encouraged when they see empowered young people go on to serve in adult roles in youth work around Australia.

"Go where people already go" might be the best advice for initiatives just starting to involve adults in service partnerships with young people. The city of Georgetown, Texas, sponsors a twice-yearly community-wide adult and youth service day. The city initiative partners with the local fellowship of Black churches on Martin Luther King Jr. Day, linking the wider community to an organized day of intentional remembrance. The partnership creates numerous intergenerational opportunities and makes reflection possible throughout the community.

If people in our community get fired up about football, we should find ways to relate youth and adult service partnerships to the sport: We can repaint the concessions area, improve the grounds, or use the occasion of a game to raise funds for an important local cause. If people are wound up about pollution in the village creek, we can create service partnerships for environmental cleanup of the waterway and surrounding banks, or collaborate on water testing and a community water-use awareness campaign. If it's an election year, political partnerships are the way to go: We can partner with youth to register new voters at the high school, conduct youth voting in the schools, and hold an open forum to introduce candidates' views to the community, with youth as the emcees.

Intangible Service: Education of the Heart

"Everybody can be great, because anybody can serve. You don't have to have a college degree to serve. You don't have to make your subject and verb agree to serve. You only need a heart full of grace, a soul generated by love."

—REV. DR. MARTIN LUTHER KING JR.

It's important to promote the intangible service that so often goes unrecognized. Many truly meaningful, spontaneous actions of service fill a direct and immediate need. But people rarely receive kudos for these actions. Peggy Contos-Hahn of Camp Hope says we need to become aware of the web of service that is going on around us all the time. "[Community awareness] is not as simple as you think. We need to celebrate service, and see how we are interdependent." (See Activity 12 on page 94.)

Every day, in small ways, we serve others, and are served by others. Whether it's done in the course of employment, family dynamics, friendship, or community, it is still service. And although it may seem a small thing to help a classmate pick up a stack of dropped books, it's a huge thing for the kid who dropped them. We need to find ways to recognize people who serve others in quiet ways.

Barbara Varenhorst describes a friendship project at Palo Alto High School in California. Upperclassmen mentor incoming grade 9 students—mentors meet their mentees, call before school starts in the fall, connect during the first two weeks of school, and keep in touch with the new students to help them find their way, if necessary. One mentor told Varenhorst, "[My mentee] wasn't doing very well in school, so I decided to study with him every night. I don't know what happened to his grades, but mine zoomed!" Varenhorst says, "[The upperclassman] was doing the mentoring because he was interested in the mentee. He gave time to his classmate. That kid will never feel worthless." She calls this "education of the heart."

Underrepresented Groups

"Being involved in your community makes not only your community stronger and better, but makes yourself stronger and better, too."

—HEATHER WILDER, 13, 2007 PRUDENTIAL SPIRIT OF COMMUNITY
AWARDS HONOREE

Service organizers often overlook some groups of youth—particularly those traditionally seen as care recipients. But all youth need opportunities to serve, and plenty of examples show it's a viable expectation, even for those who are traditionally on the receiving end of the gesture.

Sixteen-year-old Zachary Wooley—a 2007 Prudential Spirit of Community honoree from Birmingham, Alabama—can't walk, dress himself, or do his schoolwork without assistance because of his cerebral palsy. Yet Zachary joined with fellow student government officers at his school to sponsor an event that raised more than $10,000. The money was used to purchase a wheelchair and bathing chair for a girl in Poland who also lives with cerebral palsy.

PRIDE youth program in Amarillo, Texas, encourages its clients, youth in the juvenile court system, to participate in community service projects and mentoring. Team leader Jim Cameron says, "Some hard-core gang members have been visibly moved when working with physically deformed kids—especially those who are victims of crimes, such as drive-by shootings or drug deals gone bad." Cameron also says it's effective for youth in this population to help care for animals, such as dogs, that will reciprocate their affection.

Peer helpers of the Peer Information Center for Teens (PICT) in Richmond, Indiana, have included students of every academic, socioeconomic, and ability-level group in the Richmond school system—from special needs students to the class valedictorian—since 1986. Executive Director Susan Routson explains:

Some kids [in our program] can't write, but they have the gut instinct to want to help others. We give them the tools, like communication skills and resources. Everything is relative. I know of one special education student [who was a peer helper]—no one in her family had ever graduated from high school. Now she's a graduate and holds a steady job.

Service-Learning

"It's important in any service-learning activity that young people are at the helm from the beginning . . . that they choose the community they will address. Without that ability to choose, youth enthusiasm often ends. . . . We would consider an ideal service-learning setting to be one in which young people representing a range of assets and cultures are at the helm, and adults are supporting them as allies. In a community mapping activity, for example, you would see young people teaching other young people how to map their community's assets and needs, brainstorming what they anticipate they'll find, and considering ahead what they expect to be the hurdles to gathering this information. Adults would be in the room, offering advice, posing questions, and helping the process stay on track."

—MADDY WEGNER, COMMUNICATIONS DIRECTOR, NATIONAL YOUTH LEADERSHIP COUNCIL

Global initiatives celebrate service-learning by engaging youth in meaningful projects. Service-learning combines academic subject learning with community service, and requires intentional learning goals and reflection about the experience. Youth make connections between classroom learning and its application in community settings. A civic lesson might be followed up by a youth-facilitated voter registration drive. Science class research about soil and water conservation can lead to the improvement of a community's recycling program. Or an analysis of race relations could become the basis for a youth forum on the issue.

Key Service-Learning Themes

Verna Cornelia Simmons, Ed.D., and Pam Toole cite six primary service-learning themes in their service-learning diversity and equity study for the National Youth Leadership Council:

- Civic engagement and citizenship;

- Healthy youth development;

- Community development;

- Improved academic outcomes;

- Social change; and

- Understanding the interconnectedness of people.[3]

The 2004 *Growing to Greatness* survey of school principals found that only about 30 percent of schools provide service-learning opportunities to students. And since students are only about one-third as likely to participate in service projects as schools are to provide them, only 1 in 10 of the nation's students probably experience effective service-learning.[4] Still, examples are plentiful and profound.

The Carver-Scott Educational Cooperative supports youth in 15 school districts in the Minneapolis-St. Paul area who need individualized or customized education programs. Some students earn their high school diplomas by studying academic topics related to constructing or refurbishing public housing. Maddy Wegner, communications director for the National Youth Leadership Council, says the students "learn geometry by calculating the size of the drywall they might need to cut to fill a corner space under a stairway. They learn civics by studying the history of publicly subsidized housing."

Students also construct or refurbish housing for Carver and Scott counties, and often youth have previously benefited personally from the services they now provide to their communities. Wegner says:

> In the end, the young people have [earned] their high school diplomas and [gained] a range of marketable construction skills. They also have [acquired] leadership skills related to learning what the root causes of homelessness are in our culture, and understand how to address them.

Service-learning sometimes encompasses research as well. Project Cornerstone in Santa Clara County, California, sponsors a service-learning pilot program in six middle schools to facilitate youth interviews with elders. Coordinator Mary Patterson says, "We train and promote intergenerational relationship building by visiting and listening. Then they [youth] present to the elders and community members to show what they learned in this research."

Service-learning benefits both the server and the served. It gives people an opportunity to work together with others to reach a community goal—it's not charity. This requires mutually respectful community partnerships.

Many cultures integrate service as a positive aspect of passing on traditions. Communities encourage young people, at an early age, to share their money, time, and services to improve the quality of life for all. In Amish communities, neighbors work together as collective groups—in barn raisings, caring for sick neighbors, building schools and homes, and assisting with the fall harvest and spring planting. This daily, active service engages youth, as well as adults, in community life and work.

Some communities utilize traditional tribal wisdom to rejuvenate an entire population. The Eco-Walk Environmental Awareness Program, based in the Busol Watershed in the Philippines, has revived time-tested but vanishing environmental practices used by indigenous peoples. These pioneer models of community-based forest management systems sustain year-round irrigation. The program organizes activities such as tree planting, and takes children to aboriginal forests to teach them traditional wisdom about living in harmony with nature.

Children explore the watershed and learn forest conservation practices. Then they pledge to visit and take care of the trees they have planted. Children influence family members by discussing what they've learned and asking for reassurance that their trees will grow to maturity. Ramon Dacawi, Filipino resident, writer, and program manager of the project since its inception, explains:

Children teach parents about their collective responsibility . . . This experiential learning process allows children to appreciate the value of the forest in their lives and become aware of indigenous practices of forest management. To date, the children have planted over 12,200 seedlings, with a survival rate of 97 percent. They are rehabilitating the forest they will inherit one day.

Service to Peers

"Youth go to peers when they have issues, not to parents or authority figures. The goal is to make the peer [helpers] on middle school campuses more knowledgeable, informed, and mindful of the powerful role they can play in the lives of their peers."

—MARY PATTERSON, PROJECT CORNERSTONE EXECUTIVE DIRECTOR

Peer helping and peer tutoring programs have existed for decades, and their effectiveness has fostered growth in other peer programs as well, such as mentoring and conflict resolution. The National Association of Peer Programs (NAPP) helps adults establish, train, supervise, maintain, and evaluate all forms of peer programs, using a series of standards and ethics it developed to improve the quality of peer programs.

Writing in the *Peer Facilitator Quarterly,* David R. Black and his colleagues note that peer helping programs provide powerful services to many communities, and sometimes peers become "change agents." A survey of research that spans more than 25 years reveals that peer helping programs are an effective prevention strategy. Benefits to adding peer-led programs to traditional programming include greater effectiveness in decreasing illegal drug use, allowing youth to acquire self-knowledge and better attitudes, enabling peer leaders to model appropriate behaviors outside the classroom, promoting academic achievement, and establishing and enforcing conventional norms about drug and alcohol use.[5]

Although each program has its own special qualities, the mission of most peer helping programs is to train young people to listen to their peers. The Richmond, Indiana, Peer Information Center for Teens (PICT) peer helpers assist their classmates with problem solving, connect them with appropriate referral agencies, obtain accurate information, and manage conflicts. PICT serves primarily high-risk youth.

Each year 35 to 50 PICT peer helpers receive full elective credit for a semester-long training class and serve 6,000+ same-age and younger peers. They volunteer more than 10,000 hours of service per year, and PICT coordinates community service days for Richmond (Indiana) High School.

Executive Director Susan Routson says that, as a Girl Scout leader, she could see problems occurring in the lives of the girls in her troop. "I can't fix everything that is wrong in the adult community, but I can get kids to support each other," she says. "I can get a ripple effect going by teaching skillful, highly motivated older teenagers to be a support network [to their peers]. Ideally you want an adult, but you don't always get one that fits."

Barbara Varenhorst, counseling psychologist and author of several books about peer programs, says training is critical. "Of the 40 assets, about 23 to 24 are addressed directly or indirectly through the peer helping training. Young people can be asset builders for their peers."

Some students don't talk to their adult counselors—if they have problems, they turn to their friends. But their friends don't always know how to help. Training gives young people the tools they need to help their friends. Practicing skills learned in the training empowers youth. They learn confidence and gain a sense of purpose. Varenhorst says, "They take responsibility for making schools feel safer. School climate is affected."

The academic arm of peer programs witnesses similar results. Peer tutors provide a critical service to students in an educational era of higher expectations and fewer resources. Peer tutoring programs fill a void for many schools, when overscheduled teachers can't provide the extra instruction their students need to succeed. It's also a relief for busy parents, who often struggle with the schoolwork themselves.

Paula Gretzlock says peer tutors offer hope to students drowning in a subject area:

> The kids know they have people they can rely on. They're willing to ask and accept help from others. They're not just this island or entity on their own . . . The coolest thing is the kid who goes from having a tutor and seeing the benefits to wanting to be a tutor for someone else. Out of 93 tutors this year, 5 of them were that kid.

Often, peer programs become a delivery system for other asset-building initiatives. A group of motivated, well-trained, representative youth serves as an ideal pool to draw from for other school initiatives.

And current peer program participants can recruit their peers much more effectively than can adults. Transitional school activities, such as freshman orientation, also offer perfect opportunities to engage youth who are already trained and prepared to help out through peer programs.

Peer programs give youth an outlet for leadership that some wouldn't otherwise have, and help youth recognize their own talents. According to Paula Gretzlock:

> So many kids work hard and are book-smart, but haven't been leaders. They're not assertive. [In peer helping programs,] you see those kids step up in a one-to-one role, and be pretty firm and directive and take so much ownership in that relationship. Smart kids sometimes don't want to draw attention to themselves, so this is building a different aspect of their intelligence. Now those kids volunteer to facilitate training, and head up Cultural Competence Month.

Mentoring programs offer a range of services, depending upon the environment. Community programs, like Boys & Girls Clubs of America and Big Brothers Big Sisters of America, usually focus on older youth or adults building long-term relationships with younger youth. School-based programs may utilize peer mentors for one specific initiative—freshman mentors or tour guides for new students. But often, the same pool is tapped for additional specialized training in conflict resolution, peer helping, or tutoring.

In 2000, the St. Louis Job Corps trainee-led mentor program created a pool of trained mentors who served as healthy role models to other Job Corps trainees, as well as elementary and middle school students. The main focus of the program was to reduce the dropout rate of 16-, 17-, and 18-year-olds by viewing trainees as resources to each other, rather than as deficits. Mentors became positive role models and gained confidence, a sense of accomplishment, interpersonal skills, employment skills, and improved communication skills.[6]

Similarly, CLUBService—a partnership between AmeriCorps and Boys & Girls Clubs of America—funds college expenses in return for active service as mentors or for service in other areas. Elaina Ouimet, Director of Teen Services for Boys & Girls Clubs of America, says it can be a powerful experience for older members to mentor younger members. "We often find that club staff are former members themselves who gained job experience by working as junior staff members at their clubs."

Mentoring also works with grade school students as the mentors. Patty Clifford, school counselor at Pointers Run Elementary School in Howard County, Maryland, trains grade 5 students to referee grade 4 basketball and football games at recess. She introduces the referees to the entire grade 4 class, and explains that they have the responsibility to make fair calls during games at recess. "There aren't enough adults out there to watch," she says. "Peer mentors work well because the younger kids look up to the older ones."

ACTIVITY 11

Photo Opportunity for Service

Audience: Youth.

Focus: To recognize and celebrate service to others.

You will need: Several one-time-use cameras, a bulletin board, craft materials.

Before the group arrives: Choose a time of year when opportunities for community service typically arise (beginning of the school year, holidays, seasonal shifts). Generate a list of service opportunities organized by civic clubs or initiated by individual leaders.

Set the stage: Explain to students the importance of service. Discuss ways in which service helps both the youth involved and the community that is served. Ask young people to brainstorm a list of service opportunities in the community. Write down the ideas as they generate a list. Encourage youth to consider service projects both large and small. Can they think of additional acts of service that are not formally organized projects? Write these down as well.

Step 1: Give participants each a single-use camera and have each participant write their name on their camera. Ask them to photograph people engaging in community service activities over the course of a month, a week, or for just one day (such as on National and Global Youth Service Day). The time frame for the project can vary depending upon the situation. Encourage youth to write something about each photo they capture so they can remember what type of service is shown in the photos.

Step 2: At the end of the time period, collect the cameras and develop the photos, keeping students' photographs separate.

Step 3: Give youth their photos and ask them to design a bulletin board display that features their photos and celebrates the range of community service to others that they discovered.

Reflection Questions:

- What did you enjoy most about this activity?
- What service projects did you learn about that you didn't previously know of?
- What impact might this bulletin board make on our community?

(Activity adapted with permission from Communities in Schools, Houston, Texas.)

ACTIVITY 12

Simply Service

Audience: Youth.

Focus: To focus on and celebrate the intangible aspects of many acts of service.

You will need: Soft foam ball and a chair for each person, arranged in a circle.

Before the group arrives: Create a list of small acts of service that you've witnessed. These can be "random acts of kindness" or the service received from others in the course of a day at work, home, or school. Think of specific situations so you can tell a story: "A motorist lent me her cell phone so that I could call a tow truck," or "The waitress poured my coffee before I even asked for it."

Set the stage: Explain to students that we often celebrate only acts of service that involve large numbers of people and lead to big changes in the community. Remind them that we also engage in or benefit from many small acts of service every day. Share your list. Collectively, these small acts add up to a more enjoyable life for all.

Step 1: Holding the ball, share aloud an example of a random act of kindness. Pass the ball and ask youth to share their own examples.

Step 2: Next, ask youth to consider the assistance people offer them every day to help them during the course of their employment, education, or family life. Again, holding the ball, give your own example and then pass the ball to others. Ask them to back up their examples, and consider the invisible service that went into the end product: Who made the product they bought? Who constructed the building? Who transported the materials? Who organized the program? Each of these are services. Whether paid or unpaid, they all contribute to the community.

Step 3: Finally, ask youth to share the various acts of service or kindness they've offered each day. Every interaction can be viewed as a way to serve the community—helping a kid who drops his books, letting the dog into the house to relieve a family member, helping your neighbor shovel the driveway.

Reflection Questions:

- In the process of this activity, did you begin to see service in a new way? How?
- What would our community feel like if people didn't engage in these small acts of service?
- What can we do to celebrate small acts of kindness and service every day?

(Activity adapted with permission from Camp Hope, Houston, Texas.)

ACTIVITY 13

Thanks, Partner!

Audience: Youth.

Focus: To recognize and thank adults in the community who partner with youth in service projects.

You will need: Computers, thank-you cards, poster board, markers, tables and chairs.

Before the group arrives: Write a comprehensive list of adults who have partnered with youth in service projects—for National and Global Youth Service Day, in their faith communities, in youth sports programs, scouting, 4-H, or any other youth initiatives occurring in your community.

Set the stage: Explain to students that community service projects are stronger when youth and adults partner to make them happen. But often, the community is unaware of the service, or the participants in it. Adult volunteers need validation, just like youth need it.

Step 1: Share your list of adult partners in service, and ask participants if they know anyone else who should be recognized. Ask youth to sign up for individuals they would like to recognize, through a newspaper article, poster, school newspaper "ad" or announcement, or personal thank-you note.

Step 2: Help youth decide how they would like to recognize each volunteer. Youth who choose to write an article for the newspaper can pair up to recognize several adults at once, while celebrating all youth-adult partners in service. Posters might best be used to celebrate the general population of adults who serve with youth, at parent-teacher conferences, athletic events, or other gatherings adults would attend.

Step 3: Ensure that adults receive the messages sent by youth.

Reflection Questions:

- Did anything about this activity surprise you (for example, the number of adult partners who deserve recognition)?
- How do you feel when you receive recognition for something you do? How about when you don't receive recognition?
- How might this project have an impact on our school or community?

How Do We Serve Thee? Let Us Count the Ways

"Community service can change your life. When you volunteer, you think you are changing other people's lives. The ironic part about it is that you are changing your own even more."

—KYLE FREAS, 18, FOUNDER OF YOUTH TOGETHER AND A
PRUDENTIAL SPIRIT OF COMMUNITY AWARDS HONOREE

As communities begin to recognize the long-term and far-reaching impact that can be made by young people's service to others, it's becoming easier to create those experiences. Global outreach organizations provide resources that help local programs make great things happen with youth. Initiatives that would have faced logistical obstacles 10 years ago can now tap into systems with easily accessible, and sometimes free, programs and practices.

Youth-serving organizations provide support for groups focusing on youth engagement and strengthening communities. They offer many springboards for youth wanting to be responsible resources. The National Youth Leadership Council sponsors a Project Ignition program to fund creative awareness campaigns promoting teen driver safety. Each year, teams of students are awarded grants to turn their plans into action. The Campus Outreach Opportunity League maintains a search engine on its Web site for those looking for K–12 classroom lessons about service. And Youth Service America offers an online project-planning tool called Project PLAN-IT! It's designed to help young people develop a custom plan for their service project using the Internet, with an interactive series of questions and templates that guide the project-planning process. Youth can print out their plan, timeline, budget, funding proposal, press release, service-learning reflection plan, and other helpful resources.

These agencies help communities utilize service projects to mobilize young people and address local issues, develop critical thinking, and build leadership skills.

National and Global Youth Service Day is an initiative that can be incorporated into existing programs to enhance youth development goals. The organization helps community efforts by offering grants, service-learning materials, and a media and advocacy campaign.

The organization reports that it reaches millions of youth and adults every April. In 2005, 115 national partners and 50 lead agencies engaged close to 160,000 volunteers who contributed an estimated $10 million to the economy through their service. Youth plan and lead a range of projects: tutoring, collecting food and clothing, organizing social events for the elderly, restoring historic landmarks, improving the city recycling program, and coordinating a community marketing campaign to publicize the earned income tax credit.[7]

Regional initiatives exist as well. Building Youth in Basking Ridge, New Jersey, sponsors an annual "Teen Volunteer Fair" to connect local youth with organizations in need of volunteers. Organizations share with youth information about their group's mission and generate a list of volunteers for future programs and events. Kristina Roser, Community Assets coordinator, says, "It is a well-attended and valued event in the community." Similarly, Kids of Honor, Inc., in Salisbury, Maryland, strives to improve the lives and futures of struggling students by empowering them to graduate from high school. Kids of Honor supplements the activities of 19 local partner programs by engaging students and their families through service-learning activities. Youth participate in family bonding activities, sponsor food drives, clean up community landscaping, train to become peer mediators, and shadow university students.

One group of young people is helping to plan and produce a family field day and educational event for young Kids of Honor participants. Founder Paula Morris says, "Probably the most empowering portion of

Kids of Honor is the upcoming club that is yet to be named—it's being created by and for our high school kids. They want to own it, lead it, and name it, so we're empowering them to do just that."

As youth engagement gains steam, young people are beginning to ask for decision-making roles within organizations. Youth service is evolving as a means of civic engagement and activism, which reflects the values of young people.

Youth as Service Leaders

"Put the youth in the center. They have to be in every thought you have or decision you make about serving. You have to put youth first. I would ask, 'Where is the child in the budget?' or 'How does the decision to build this building impact young people?'"

—PEGGY CONTOS-HAHN, CAMP HOPE, HOUSTON, TEXAS

Not all service projects are organized by a club or coordinated by committee. Sometimes individual youth just "get jazzed," and in the right environment, they accomplish remarkable things.

When Josh, a sophomore at New Richmond High School in Wisconsin, suggested the SPARK Peer Tutors could start a middle school program, his advisor was hesitant to jump on the idea. But the group had previously taken on other leadership projects in addition to tutoring, and the high school tutors were already helping middle school youth. It seemed there was sufficient need to warrant establishing a separate program. Although his advisor liked the idea, she was concerned about overextending herself. But Josh wasn't really asking anything of his advisor—he simply posed a project idea to the group, and several members seemed quite interested. The students had previously demonstrated their collective ability to reach goals in other projects. So, rather than communicate all the idea's potential roadblocks to the group, Josh's advisor decided to serve as a sounding board and counselor, and she ultimately empowered the students to find the answers to the questions they had. That's really all they needed or wanted.

Within months, this small committee of focused SPARK members identified and connected with interested middle school staff, wrote and received a grant to fund their project, led a training for new grade 8 tutors, and handed over the peer tutoring program to the new middle school advisor.

How often we assume that the ideas generated by youth are just going to add more responsibilities to our plate. It can be a natural tendency for overworked educators and youth workers to shoot down youth suggestions because they're too stressed to handle the extra responsibility. The key is for youth to earn our trust so that we feel comfortable allowing it to become *their* extra responsibility, rather than ours.

Sometimes a personal challenge inspires a young person. At age 9, Chase Kroll of Dover, Delaware, was diagnosed with juvenile diabetes. At age 12, he started a newsletter for other kids with diabetes to inform and make connections between kids who had the condition. Chase's newsletter, *Despite Diabetes*, provided facts, tips, and profiles of youth and adults who thrive, despite diabetes.

His inspiration came from a younger diabetic student at his school who could only drink water with lunch because of specific restrictions in his diet. Chase decided to raise money to buy Crystal Light, a carbohydrate-free flavored water supplement, and give it to the younger boy for his lunchtime drink by asking for donations in an informational newsletter.

With the help of his mom and teacher, Chase applied for and received a grant, and his classmates helped him prepare the newsletter for distribution to teachers, school nurses, and medical clinics in all 50 states. The donations he received from people who read the newsletters were used to purchase Crystal Light packets for his friend and also supported the work of the American Diabetes Association.

People wrote letters to Chase to tell him how they felt when they were first diagnosed with diabetes, and how they have handled the disease throughout their lives. He received more than 65 letters from diabetics of all ages throughout the world and published them in a book, *When I Got Diabetes: Letters to Chase*. Chase recognized a need in his community, because it was a personal need as well, and he found a way to fill that need.

Sometimes youth overcome obstacles to inspire others to do the same. When Kyle Freas moved from Austin to Plano, Texas, in 1999, he was a sad and angry kid. Kyle had been thrown against a chair by a teacher when he was in grade 4. "I had completely shut down," he says.

After learning about Kyle's situation, his new principal handpicked a teacher for him. Kyle would later say that this new teacher changed his life. "She took me to the Stars game, and we got to sit in her box. She came to my soccer games and basketball games and watched me. She made me come alive again," he says. "By November, I had improved so much that I was voted student council president."

Kyle started a nonprofit program called Plano Youth Together (now called Youth Together) that partners with schools to teach children about community service. His first project was Operation Backpack, which was prompted by his earlier, painful classroom experience. "When children are involved in abusive situations, they are often removed from their homes with only the clothes on their backs. We supplied backpacks and supplies to these children so that they could return to school ready to [have] a normal routine," Kyle says. "We are helping ourselves when we help each other. We change our lives when we start to volunteer."

Youth as Philanthropists

"Adults have been involving kids in fund-raising drives for decades. What is new is empowering kids to be the leaders of social change."

—DEBORAH SPAIDE, AUTHOR OF *TEACHING YOUR KIDS TO CARE*

When Danny Butler was 12 years old, his parents gave him the book *Free the Children*, the story of Craig Kielburger, who, as a 12-year-old, founded an organization to combat child labor around the world. Danny's dad, Scott, says, "Our goal in giving Dan the book was to show him that youth have the power to change the world."

Danny was inspired. His dad relates, "He realized that his own life in this country is great compared to [the lives of] children around the world, and this position implies an obligation to help others. He finished the book realizing that not only could he make a difference but also realizing that he had a moral obligation to do so."

Danny's parents asked him what service he'd like to do for his community. They thought he'd create a relatively easy local project. But Danny had visited the Free the Children Web site and wanted to raise money to build and outfit a school in rural China. His dad says, "He told us he wanted to raise $5,000. I was a little shocked by the goal. I worried about what would happen if he didn't make it or if it became too hard. When I asked about that possibility, he responded, 'It'll take as long as it takes, and I'll get it done.'"

Danny, now a teenager, organized a multifamily garage sale, a karate tournament coordinated and judged by youth, presentations to local organizations, candle sales, and a student council fund-raiser. In less than a year, he met his goal. A day after reaching the $5,000 mark, another check arrived in the mail. When Danny's dad asked him what he would do with the money, since he'd already raised the funds needed to build the school, he simply said, "I guess I'll just build another one."

Danny learned countless leadership skills and is currently serving on an Omaha city advisory board as a youth representative. His dad says, "As I look back at the last year, I realize it has been a real rite of passage for him. This has been life changing for him. He realizes his own power to change the world, and the obligation he has to do so. He's realized how good his own life is, and he is far less materialistic and far more grateful."

Danny's project illustrates a relatively new concept in youth service—youth philanthropy. While most youth don't found money-giving charities themselves, as Craig Kielburger, Ryan Hreljac, or Danny Butler did, it's becoming more common for youth to serve as board members of existing youth charities. Youth philanthropy uniquely strengthens grassroots programs that impact young people. Funding builds the momentum that's needed in order for initiatives to flourish. Youth philanthropy encompasses a range of participants without requiring personal wealth. This broader definition builds on an internal motivation of collective responsibility, viewing philanthropists also as those who contribute their time, talents, and treasure for the common good.

More than 250 youth philanthropy initiatives exist in foundations, community organizations, and schools nationwide, and in 2000, youth-led groups gave between $5 million and $10 million in grants. Youth philanthropists serve multiple purposes for nonprofit boards and other charities. They raise funds, offer grants, solicit and evaluate proposals, and oversee funded projects. Most youth philanthropy initiatives involve both youth and adults in decision making, and give young people the final authority in awarding grants.

Youth philanthropy allows young people to actively change their own lives and the lives of those around them. It shifts our understanding of charity. This philosophy promotes the idea that all people can be appreciated for their unique skills and abilities when they're offered authentic opportunities to contribute.

Like other groups, philanthropic boards benefit from youth participation as well. Youth possess the unique ability to "think outside the box" and provide a new perspective on issues. This makes them creative problem solvers when designing solutions for community problems. Youth philanthropy gives young people an outlet for expressing their talents and allocating their time to affect society in a profound way.

It's All Good

With so much need, wise communities tap one of their most valuable assets—young people. Too often, these bright, energetic people are never asked to serve. Whether you organize a group of youth carolers to entertain at the local nursing home, or follow the lead of a middle school student who thinks something should be done about the trash in the park, or serve as a Board of Review member for the Eagle Scout who might be a future president . . . it's all good.

Mark, a blogger, expresses the sad but honest truth about what many adults believe about youth: "Sometimes I look at the youth of this country, and I wonder and worry about the future. Undoubtedly, I'm making sweeping generalizations, and exceptions exist, but I see it in the news, and I see it myself every day. It seems like our society, generally, has become exceptionally self-centered and lazy."

An unexpected event changed Mark's point of view:

I was finishing shoveling the sidewalk when I looked up and saw the neighbor kids coming over to help me shovel the driveway. I was shocked. The five of them were eager to help and took right to it with zeal. Their kindness and thoughtfulness was unsolicited. They just came over to help me for the sake of helping. Wow. They could have been watching TV. They could have been building snowmen. They could have been sledding. Needless to say, they proved me wrong about today's youth. I suspect they are one of the exceptions that I admitted to above, but they still made my hope and outlook for the future much brighter.

The simple act of five kids shoveling snow redefined an adult's entire perception of youth as a whole—from viewing them as a cause of problems to seeing them as a source of solutions. They challenged a stereotype without saying a word. This is one of the benefits of service. It transforms a young person from passive recipient to active service provider. In theory, these roles are worlds apart, but in reality, they're just a step away.

ACTIVITY 14

Create a Catalog of Service

Audience: Youth.

Focus: To create a resource of service opportunities for youth and adults wishing to serve the community.

You will need: Telephones, computers, and printers.

Before the group arrives: Generate a "starter list" of service opportunities in the community, along with contact names and numbers, if available. Organize a possible distributor for the service catalog—community education, Chamber of Commerce, or religious organizations might be a good start.

Set the stage: Explain that more young people would probably participate in service opportunities if they knew what was available. Explain that the group will be creating a service catalog for the community—a listing and description of service opportunities, contact names, and numbers.

Step 1: First generate a comprehensive list of service opportunities—both large and small. Show your premade list and encourage youth to brainstorm additions to the list based on their knowledge and experiences. If they know contact names and numbers, include this information now.

Step 2: Once the list is complete, ask youth to sign up to research individual service opportunities. Youth will interview people in charge of service projects to get accurate descriptions, dates and times of service, particular needs, and contact information.

Step 3: After researching the service opportunities, each youth will type short entries for the service catalog, including all pertinent information. Organize and alphabetize the listing, print a copy, and deliver it to the agency that will distribute the final product.

Reflection Questions:

- What surprised you about this project?
- What service projects did you learn about that you didn't previously know existed?
- What impact might this catalog have on our community?
- What could we do to produce this catalog more effectively next time?

ACTIVITY 15

Levels of Service

Audience: Youth.

Focus: To recognize and celebrate all levels of service, and encourage goal setting.

You will need: Chart paper, markers, tables that seat approximately six participants, whiteboard.

Before the group arrives: Generate a "starter list" of service opportunities in the community, for personal reference during the activity.

Set the stage: Explain that service is good and necessary in the community. At different times in our lives, we're more or less able to give, and we give in different ways. The way we serve is less important than the fact that we *do* serve. And when we make a strong commitment to service, we can benefit our community and ourselves in large ways.

Step 1: Ask table groups to create three columns on their chart paper—one each for monthly, weekly, and daily acts of service.

Step 2: Create sample columns on the whiteboard and write "starter" examples on your own list. Ask youth to brainstorm potential and actual service opportunities they might engage in. Write them in the appropriate column as youth say them.

Step 3: When the groups are finished discussing, ask each participant to write three specific goals related to service based on the columns generated and her or his current ability to commit. Ask participants to share their goals with the larger group.

Reflection Questions:

- In the process of this activity, did you begin to see service in a new way? How?
- What would our community feel like if no one took on the small acts of service? The large ones?
- What can we do to celebrate all acts of service every day?

Moving from "Me" to "We"

- Volunteer. You'll connect with like-minded adults and serve as a role model for youth.

- Ask a young person to join you. Partnering can be the most powerful aspect of service.

- Ask an adult to join you. Once they feel a sense of personal satisfaction, they'll be back for more.

- Recognize and thank people when you witness their service. Write a thank-you card. Recognition is a powerful motivator.

- Be a resource for an inspired youth with a big idea.

- Participate in or lead a service project for an organization of which you're a member.

- Take aside someone you know who is involved in community philanthropy. Ask her or him how youth are involved in the organization.

- Join in service on National and Global Youth Service Day.

- Invite your neighbors to a ditch cleanup party.

- Use your everyday examples of service to inspire a new norm. Open the door for someone carrying a heavy load. Mow your neighbor's sideyard, or shovel the driveway when your neighbor is unable to do so. Opportunities abound.

Did You Know?

Seventeen-year-old Bridget Alldritt of Chisago City, Minnesota, co-founded an annual summer camp for children stricken with ulcerative colitis and Crohn's disease. She has suffered from chronic ulcerative colitis since she was nine years old, so she and her mother developed a six-day, all-volunteer summer camp that gives children with colitis and Crohn's disease the chance to have medically supervised fun at a relatively low cost. Bridget was a 2007 Prudential Spirit of Community Awards honoree.

4

ENSURING A SAFE WORLD FOR YOUNG PEOPLE

"Never underestimate the absolutely profound impact [you] can have on the world by working with youth. Miracles happen. [I] would encourage anybody who works with children to never give up. And never underestimate what they can do."

—MICHAEL DORN, AUTHOR, *WEAKFISH: BULLYING THROUGH THE EYES OF A CHILD*

Perhaps your community is like this one: Neighborhood watch signs are posted in windows. Seniors supervise children at school bus stops and crosswalks. Drivers follow the speed limit because neighbors have rallied for neon pedestrian signs and caution flags at busy crossings. Families host alcohol-free parties for their kids' friends. Parents know what's happening in the lives of their children's peers, take turns supervising each other's children, and model safe choices by driving sober, wearing bike helmets, and speaking up when they see a dangerous situation. Schools organize all-night prom and graduation parties to help students make safe choices. City councils help youth make positive choices with their time by promoting activities like beach parties, dances, and skateboarding at community parks. And community members fight crime, pressuring their politicians to provide resources when problems arise.

But not all communities enjoy this Mayberry-like environment, and there's no doubt that safety is a serious problem for many youth:

- Only 51 percent of youth say they feel safe at home, at school, and in the neighborhood.

- Thirty percent of youth report one or more incidents of physical abuse, and 29 percent report they've been a victim of violence one or more times in the past two years.

- Thirty-four percent of youth report having engaged in three or more incidents of violence in the past 12 months.[1]

- Thirty-seven percent of students say they know another student who might use a gun at school, and 8 percent have thought of shooting someone themselves.

- Seventy-five percent of middle school and high school students fear a shooting will occur in their school, and 25 percent state that students can easily get access to a gun.[2]

Every day, television news captures the stories about worldwide dangers, from countries torn apart by war, epidemics, and drought to severely impoverished children working under appalling conditions around the world. Developed countries struggle to address unsafe situations as well—gang violence, school shootings, homelessness, child abuse and neglect, and the terrible aftermath of natural disasters. Safety concerns continually present themselves in multiple forms— threats to physical, emotional, and health-related safety.

Even as early as the 1950s, psychologist Abraham Maslow argued that until the physiological and safety needs of humans are addressed, people have little chance of meeting higher-level needs, such as belongingness, self-esteem, and self-actualization. Sociological research demonstrates that neighborhoods with scarce emotional and physical resources face multiple threats to the social, educational, and developmental outcomes of the children who live there. In short, young people who are concerned about their personal safety—because of war, neighborhood violence, abuse, or bullying—are often hard-pressed to reach other goals.

Most would agree there's a lot of work to be done globally to address war, drugs, poverty, child welfare, health, and race relations. Many of these issues are so much larger, and more deeply rooted, than can possibly be addressed in a book of this scope. And what do they have to do with empowerment?

Consider this: A mother brings her toddler to a neighbor's back-yard barbecue. They join the other guests on the deck, only to discover the deck has no railing. All afternoon, the mother chases after her child, holds her in her lap, and repeatedly says "no." The child struggles against her mother's embrace because she wants to explore, to peer over the edge of the deck and see what is so exciting that she isn't allowed to discover it.

The same gathering, protected by a safe railing and a gate, would produce an entirely different experience for the mother and her young child. The toddler could leave her mother's side, mingle with guests, explore her surroundings, and learn about the playthings within the confined area. She could walk directly to the railing. She could wonder about what lies beyond—with her eyes, her ears, and her voice. She could ask questions to learn more.

And she could do all this safely.

Young children can safely explore and learn when they are given an appropriate environment in which to do so. Likewise, when older youth are given freedom within firm boundaries, they're able to learn responsibility, make choices without disastrous consequences, and learn from their mistakes without becoming a statistic. We don't tell a responsible 6th grader not to handle a kitchen knife—we teach her how to hold it safely. And we don't tell a 16-year-old not to drive a car—we teach him how to do it safely. In order to empower youth to make wise choices, discover their world, and learn from their mistakes, we as a society— parents and educators, neighbors and family—must provide the safe environment within which appropriate learning can occur.

Taken one step further, we must see youth as stakeholders in their schools and communities—people whose voices are heard in a genuine effort to recognize dangers and find solutions to the safety challenges facing all of us.

WHAT VALUE DOES YOUR COMMUNITY PLACE ON CREATING A SAFE ENVIRONMENT FOR YOUTH?

The following actions and attitudes characterize a community that creates a sense of safety for its youth. Does your community make the following characteristics of safety at home, at school, and in the neighborhood a priority?

ALWAYS SOMETIMES NEVER

☐ ☐ ☐ Adults and youth participate in discussions about safety in the school and community and potential solutions to danger.

☐ ☐ ☐ Families feel safe in their neighborhoods, and don't feel the need to limit their activities because of crime.

☐ ☐ ☐ Residents work to keep their community safe by reaching out to their neighbors and monitoring suspicious activities.

☐ ☐ ☐ Residents rally to get the resources and support necessary to thwart violence.

☐ ☐ ☐ Courts employ proactive strategies to educate and foster communication while enforcing laws.

☐ ☐ ☐ Parents connect with each other's families, creating a web of information to guide their kids in making safe choices.

☐ ☐ ☐ Community sponsors initiatives and safe activities to involve youth in fun, safe, and healthy choices.

☐ ☐ ☐ Parents engage neighborhood youth in healthy, safe, and fun activities.

☐ ☐ ☐ Schools sponsor training to teach bullying interventions, and staff members identify and intervene in bullying situations.

☐ ☐ ☐ Schools and other community organizations adopt weapon-free and drug-free policies.

☐ ☐ ☐ School and civic leaders ask for youth input to create a safer environment for kids.

☐ ☐ ☐ Police act as partners in the education of young people.

☐ ☐ ☐ Trained peer helpers and other students serve as eyes and ears of awareness in bullying situations.

Reprinted with permission from *Empowering Youth: How to Encourage Young Leaders to Do Great Things,* by Kelly Curtis, M.S. Copyright © 2008 by Search Institute, Minneapolis, Minnesota, 800-888-7828, www.search-institute.org. All rights reserved.

Building a Foundation
for a Safe Neighborhood

*"I was known in the community. Everyone had an
eye on me and on what my future looked like."*

—DEMETRIO L. BEACH, CHARACTER EDUCATOR, GRAYSONVILLE, MARYLAND

When individuals make safety a priority, we hear about parents and neighbors "taking back their community." They want drug-free schools, weapon-free streets, and clean, safe homes for well-fed families who receive appropriate medical care. Empowered neighbors make serious changes in their communities, often with few resources. But they can make even more progress in partnership with others.

Organizations find ways to work within dangerous environments. Boys & Girls Clubs of America partnered with the Pillsbury Company to fund pilot programs that provided safe, central meeting sites for youth and volunteers. Ed Mishrell, vice president of Boys & Girls Clubs of America, says, "One of the challenges is that a lot of the kids that need our program the most are living in communities where it might be uncomfortable to knock on their doors. The idea was that the club would be a convening place to make those connections."

The club organized monthly outings, invited kids and volunteers to meet at the club, and transported the whole group in a bus. This attention to detail removed many of the potential barriers to establishing positive relationships between youth and volunteers. Mishrell says, "Kids who have grown up in the program are now [the ones] providing services for it. [They have] an opportunity to be role models for kids who are growing up in the same circumstances."

Similarly, on an international scale, the Jordan-based nonprofit organization Questscope empowers marginalized groups by linking street children and at-risk youth with mentors in Jordan, Lebanon, the Syrian Arab Republic, and the United Kingdom. The organization also involves youth in mentoring programs, informal education, small-business projects, youth leadership development, and direct referrals to institutions that can help them. Curt Rhodes, Questscope president and international director, writes on the organization's Web site about his experience with his first mentor more than 40 years ago: "I can still remember the interest in his eyes as he listened to whatever a 14-year-old had to talk about. I have forgotten the topics of my talking, but I have never forgotten the intensity of his listening."[3]

A study conducted by Rhodes demonstrated the effectiveness of reinforcing positive behavior. Adults respected and rewarded new and proactive roles undertaken by youth, and took time to understand the points of view offered by the children about their own circumstances. Researchers noted, "Their [previously negative] behaviors made perfect sense to them, given the pressures they endured."

Even without organized programs, parents and neighbors can significantly impact safety, but they may need help to learn how to reach out to kids. The notion of "stranger danger" impedes efforts of adults relating to kids. Karen Atkinson, coordinator for Children First in St. Louis Park, Minnesota, says:

> Neighbors need to mobilize and get to know one another. Especially with young children, you get to know the family, not just the child. You can also feel free to greet a child as you pass, but don't approach a child you don't know, unless a parent is present.

Senior citizens sometimes organize efforts as well. For example, they might supervise children while they wait at bus stops. "A member of our senior center shared that he and his wife hold the keys of several neighbors' homes, most of which have both parents working." He told Atkinson, "If the children are locked out, they know they can get a key from us. If they feel scared being home alone, they know they can come to our house. This only happens once or twice a year, but I think they take comfort just knowing we are there."

These ongoing connections between adults and youth are worth the effort. A study by Students Against Destructive Decisions (SADD) shows that teens who identify at least one influential, natural mentor in their lives report that they have a higher sense of self-esteem and are more likely to take risks that affect their lives in positive ways.

Safe School

"In looking for ways to prevent violence, our children and adolescents are as much our teachers as [they are] our students, and they need to be both counseled and listened to." [4]

—DAVID DEREZOTES, DEB ASHTON, AND TRACIE HOFFMAN, THE VOICES
PROJECT, UNIVERSITY OF UTAH SCHOOL OF SOCIAL WORK

Although many forms of violence have existed in schools for a long time, the well-publicized school homicides of the past decade have spurred large-scale concern about the reality of serious school violence. This has resulted in nationwide study and debate about the best ways to manage safety issues in schools, while at the same time keeping a productive learning environment in place.

Schools of thought sometimes vary widely among school officials, parents, educators, and safety management professionals. But often, in the frantic shuffle to curb violence, a safety committee convenes, discusses, brainstorms, and makes a decision without ever bringing youth to the table. And the solution adults identify for greater safety might be very different from what young people would suggest. A compelling argument for asking students about their perception of an unsafe situation is that youth who feel their views are valued by adults may be less likely to act violently.

Bullying is currently a widespread school safety concern. In recent years, society has recognized the long-term negative impact of bullying and the need for intervention. School officials now identify as serious and destructive situations that were formerly seen as accepted rites of passage. Diligent attention must be given to this behavior. It's common for some children to endure chronic, daily bullying, leading to thoughts of dropping out of school, suicide, or getting a weapon and retaliating. One study found that 12 to 18 percent of children are bullied every day but never tell an adult. [5]

School violence expert Michael Dorn says these are the children who most need an adult to reach out to them. Dorn insists adults need to be vigilant when it comes to youth bullying. They must care and be alert, and become educated about effective approaches and investigation techniques. What appears to be a simple incident involving hitting or name-calling may actually be far more serious. Many kids who are being chronically bullied only tell someone about it once. Dorn says, "They may report one incident, but do not necessarily tell you what has been going on for the last three months."[6]

But children can also change the way they interact with each other. Erik Laursen, past president of Strength-Based Services International, suggests empowering members within a group to foster a commitment to caring for and helping one another. He says if kids endanger themselves or others, we shouldn't necessarily blame the teacher for not witnessing the event. Instead, we need to train other children so they know how to react and help peers be safe.

Laursen proposes giving youth as much responsibility as possible to cultivate caring peer environments, and says that adult interaction should be indirect, rather than command attention. If classmates aren't listening when a peer reads aloud, Laursen says it is more effective for the teacher to say, "Does Sharon have everyone's attention?" This approach creates an environment of peer interdependence, rather than adult dependence.[7]

Crime and Punishment

"Communities, cities, and countries are oozing hope. I'm in a unique position to bring back the hope—to be strategic and think way ahead, and partner and support and speak the same language. Others are leading the charge too. We're supporting them—coming together as partners to promote the assets. As a result we'll champion hundreds of thousands of kids."

—WARD CLAPHAM, CHIEF OF THE ROYAL CANADIAN MOUNTED POLICE,
COMMENTING ON POSITIVE POLICING IN RICHMOND, BRITISH COLUMBIA

The most effective empowering communities include all stakeholders in reaching goals for youth. This includes law enforcement and judicial arms of the community. Richmond, British Columbia, a city with under 200,000 residents in the greater Vancouver area, boasts the most diverse population in Canada, with an approximately 70 percent nonwhite population. Richmond adopted "comprehensive policing" and the positive ticket approach as one of the main duties of its police officers. This transformational change in policing involves the entire community in positive recognition.

Positive tickets double as coupons for free goods and services from local establishments. When a police officer notices a young person engaging in a positive behavior—helping a child across the street, caring for a wounded animal, offering to assist a senior citizen in carrying groceries—the officer tickets the youth in a positive way.

It works. In the first three years of this initiative, the city of Richmond experienced a 41 percent reduction in youth crime. Ward Clapham says, "This means 1,056 kids per year who are no longer murdered, drug addicts, or burglars that we have to worry about as a community, and that are on a positive track instead of a negative track."

The police department integrates the 40 Developmental Assets framework and youth-related goals into its five-year strategic plan. In a comprehensive approach with long-term vision and strategy, it applies equal importance to all five aspects of policing: investigation, enforcement, protection, intelligence, and prevention education.

The school board, health department, social agencies, and the city of Richmond use a common language structured around the assets. And the Richmond police department believes in the importance of prevention and education, so it utilizes youth officers who work directly with young people in the schools. Clapham says, "If we develop trust and relationships, they'll have the courage to talk to us and help us do our job better."

Each year, the community purchases eight season hockey tickets. Two plain clothes police officers invite six different youth to attend each game with them. Clapham says, "Every year, over 500 Richmond young people get personal quality time with a youth officer [who acts] as a buddy, coach, mentor, and friend."

In the 1990s, Clapham tried to implement this sports-attendance program in Calgary, Canada, but was challenged by old-school peers who questioned the cost. In Richmond, the program was nearly canceled because of similar negative pressure. But then Clapham attended a game with a young person:

It wasn't until [the young man] felt comfortable and started chatting with me that I found out his dad had died recently, and he needed to talk about it. We ended up not even watching the game. It was transformational for me.

That's when Clapham became so passionate about positive policing. "I found the courage to swim upstream against the strongest current." He thinks we're maturing as a society, and can now recognize the value of a long-term investment of time and energy in relationships with young people. Officers now look out for kids who are making positive choices—not just the negative ones. They still investigate and punish, but Clapham says, "We can deal with it with a different set of eyes. There is hope. It's about reframing and rethinking."

Restorative justice is a strategy based in native tribal practice and used by courts throughout the world. Courts hold youth personally accountable for their actions, and give victims an opportunity to participate in delivery of the consequences. The facilitator explains the process and ground rules to the victim and the offender separately, and ultimately holds conferences with all parties together in a civilized, safe environment in which everyone is heard. Although society still needs the traditional justice system, courts are sometimes more effective by balancing the two philosophies.

As a circuit court judge of the Wisconsin Court of Appeals, Edward Brunner spearheaded restorative justice practices in Barron County, Wisconsin. "Restorative justice is looking at the justice system and crime as an injury—an offense against the community. When you have an injury, you try to heal it—to find a way to heal the victim, make the victim whole, the community whole, and provide an opportunity to give the offender a chance to redeem himself and hopefully rehabilitate," says Brunner.

Schools in Barron County adopted restorative practices in their disciplinary codes, and also in morning circles, where teachers and administrators facilitate disputes using restorative justice principles. Brunner notes that since 2000, the Barron County courts have experienced an 80 percent reduction in school referrals and a 60 percent reduction in juvenile delinquency cases.

The first case involving restorative justice in Brunner's community was a heated one. Four teenagers stole turkeys from a local farm and slaughtered them inside the school, watching the dying turkeys run around and make a gory mess. Even though the youth readily admitted to their acts when caught, residents were very angry. Brunner says, "The more it festered, the angrier they got. People wanted to take away their scholarships—to not let them graduate."

The boys' parents finally said, "Let's punish them, but [don't] ruin their lives over this." A facilitator began the restorative justice process, with 28 community members attending the first meeting. They listened to the explanation of the ground rules, and one of the participants told Brunner, "This isn't going to work—they're all too angry."

When the youth were finally brought together with the community members, the teenagers explained the incident and answered questions, talked about how this had affected them, and sincerely apologized. Then one of the youth personally told each person how sorry he was for having hurt the community in this way. Brunner says the man who was most vocal about punishing the boys said, "After what happened tonight, I will always remember you for what you did tonight, not for what you did then." The whole group was in tears.

The court fined the youth and they made restitution, paying for cleanup and damages. Brunner says, "It had a happy ending. This seems to be a healthier way to handle it for everyone involved."

Safe Roads

Not all safety issues are related to violence or crime. Many safety concerns arise from a lack of education about proper choices. But even without violence, danger is still present.

Traffic accidents continue to be the leading cause of death for 15- to 20-year-olds. In 2003, 3,657 U.S. drivers in this age group were killed, and an additional 308,000 were injured in motor vehicle crashes. According to the National Association of Peer Programs, nearly 31 percent of teen drivers killed in crashes in 2003 had been drinking and 74 percent were not wearing safety belts.[8] Seventeen percent of youth report they've driven after drinking or ridden with a drinking driver three or more times in the last 12 months.[9]

The National Organization for Youth Safety (NOYS) is a coalition of youth organizations focusing on youth safety and health. It offers local organizations an opportunity to collaborate to create strong programs, through youth empowerment and leadership, and partnerships that enhance safe and healthy lifestyles among youth.

NOYS sponsors National Youth Traffic Safety Month each May, a youth-led campaign to educate peers about the importance of road safety. It raises awareness about road traffic injuries and the risks for young drivers, and also promotes the use of bicycle helmets and safety belts, prevention of impaired driving and speeding, and investment in road infrastructure. Similarly, youth educator campaigns, such as Think First, remind teenagers about the serious consequences for poor choices following prom or graduation parties each spring.

Often empowerment isn't much more than effective training—giving young people the tools to make better choices for themselves. Rather than shielding youth from danger, we need to teach them how to handle the danger. And role modeling is critical. Young drivers need to buckle up, follow the speed limit, and not make distracting choices, but it's difficult to send this message when youth see adults using their cell phones, applying makeup, and eating while operating a vehicle.

Timothy Smith, author of *Crashproof Your Kids*, says that parents need to teach kids critical skills that aren't covered in driver education programs, such as understanding how their vehicles work, driving defensively, and being alert and attentive while driving. He writes, "Parents have the ultimate responsibility to ensure that their teenagers develop safe driving skills and behaviors. But too many—either underestimating their role or lacking effective methods—have failed to help equip their teens to handle the single most dangerous thing they will ever do, at their most risky age."[10]

Side-by-side partnerships between kids and parents will help youth learn how to handle a dangerous situation in a vehicle. In northern Wisconsin, where icy roads endanger drivers for five months each year, parents often teach their kids how to maneuver on ice-covered parking lots or frozen-over lakes. Instead of orchestrating the lives of teenagers so that they never come into contact with an unsafe environment, we need to empower them to know what to do in an unsafe situation.

In addition to this critical parent role, empowered youth can help each other be safe on the road. The JourneySafe outreach program based in Laguna Beach, California, educates teens and parents about the inherent risks and responsibilities associated with being a teen driver and teen passenger. Through informational materials, teen-to-teen programs, and presentations to schools and youth groups, JourneySafe promotes and teaches a "positive peer pressure—friends protecting friends" concept.

According to JourneySafe's Web site (www.journeysafe.org), recent teen surveys show that 67 percent of teens admit to having experienced feelings of being unsafe while driving with friends, yet only 45 percent would be willing to say something to the driver:

> *Rather than as their ticket to freedom, we want teens to view the privilege of a driver's license as their initiation into the adult world of assuming responsibility for others.*

Safe Health

Safety also encompasses health, and there are many ways for our bodies to be unsafe. Drug use, risky sexual behaviors, and poor food choices put bodies at risk for disease and poor quality of life. When it comes to health, knowledge empowers.

Erie's Promise, an alliance for youth based in Erie, Pennsylvania, coordinates a "Red Wagons, Red Flags" initiative that helps youth from 15 school districts create awareness campaigns aimed at preventing risky teen behaviors. One of the projects focuses on HIV/AIDS awareness. In a collaborative effort, Erie County health agencies, college staff and students, teen educators, and people living with the disease lead interactive awareness presentations.

The program teaches high school youth to identify warning signs and avoid situations that may put their health at risk. It provides teachers with HIV education programs and invites peer educators to teach them. According to program coordinators, demand for HIV testing and counseling has increased significantly among this age group at the Erie County Department of Health.

Another prevention initiative, Yellow Ribbon International Suicide Prevention Program, is a community-based program using a universal public health approach. It helps communities empower and educate adults and youth by distributing Yellow Ribbon "Ask 4 Help" cards, which give youth in crisis the words they need to ask adults for help if they're feeling suicidal and give others the "what to do next" steps. The cards are business-sized and include suicide prevention hotline phone numbers. Adults are encouraged to respond appropriately and immediately if a young person says to them, "I need to use my Yellow Ribbon."

According to the program's Web site, www.yellowribbon.org:

> The Yellow Ribbon Program is based on the premise that suicide is not about death, but rather about ending pain, and it's OK to ask for help. Yellow Ribbon cards are distributed and carried as a simple, effective tool [for teens] to use to ask for help when feelings of suicide arise.

Although the topic was once taboo, communities and school districts now sponsor Yellow Ribbon activities, distribute "Ask 4 Help" cards, and generate awareness of suicide prevention strategies. Some communities sponsor adult trainings in suicide prevention, and print on the card a list of local crisis resources available to teens. By learning about and discussing this critical public health topic, people are empowered by knowing the first step to take in handling a potential suicide situation.

Safe Differences

"[My teacher] said that the greatest problem people have is that they don't understand each other, not out of spite, but often out of ignorance."

—EVAN APPLEMAN, 18, PRUDENTIAL SPIRIT OF COMMUNITY
AWARDS HONOREE, INDIANAPOLIS, INDIANA

Prejudice has the power to divide like nothing else does, and when it's left unchecked, it can become an unmanageable monster. Reservoir High School—a new school made up of youth from previously over-crowded schools in Howard County, Maryland—seized an opportunity to be proactive in combating prejudice at school. To help the diverse and somewhat disparate communities come together at the new school, teaching staff used a group model called Project CommUNITY.

Representative youth participated in team-building exercises off-campus to create a sense of community and to set positive norms for student behavior, and they prepared to filter their learning back into the school. Principal Addie Kaufman says:

> We took students and staff members on overnight retreats where we spent time building bonds, learning about each other, and developing plans for building community and a positive school climate. After the first retreat, students began to lead activities at other retreats. This was a terrific way to empower students.

One of the critical discussions centered on norms of safety. Staff members asked students, "How will you stay physically, emotionally, and psychologically safe?" After processing other questions like this one, youth returned to the school prepared to live out the actions that would allow safety to become a reality. Project CommUNITY graduate Christine Vidmar says:

> Because of the diverse population in my high school, we had a lot of work to do in order to create a safe, healthy, respectful, and open-minded environment. These opportunities have provided me with an open mind and willingness to accept all types of people. My friends come from every different background imaginable.

"Safe Staff"

"Our GLBT youth are more comfortable now. They don't have to pretend to be what they're not."

—PAULA GRETZLOCK, SCHOOL COUNSELOR, NEW RICHMOND
HIGH SCHOOL, NEW RICHMOND, WISCONSIN

Even in communities that have an apparent lack of outward diversity, it's important to encourage and teach people to accept differences among people. "Safe Staff" is a program that supports schools in their efforts to train teaching staff to be accepting of differences in students' sexual preferences and identity, and make themselves available to listen to GLBT youth. In-house employees or local agencies facilitate in-service trainings, and staff members display Safe Staff rainbow decals on their office windows as a sign of invitation where GLBT youth can feel safe.

The visual recognition of the Safe Staff and Safe Zone window stickers is very high. Kids are savvy and know what the stickers represent. Paula Gretzlock, a school counselor at New Richmond (Wisconsin) High School, says:

> *Every staff member that's gone through the training and has displayed Safe Zone materials has had at least one person come [talk] to them. Now we're past the point of people reporting to me who comes to talk to them.*

In a schoolwide homeroom activity, youth brainstorm aloud a list of derogatory comments or words related to diverse groups, which helps them make a direct connection between the words they use and the bias that is sometimes behind those words. In classroom activities and lessons that teach tolerance of differences between the self and others, Gretzlock makes a point of directly addressing GLBT diversity awareness, rather than just lumping sexuality together with other forms of discrimination. She says, "The hardest ones for the kids to say are those related to sexuality."

Gretzlock introduced Safe Staff to a relatively conservative faculty. She says, "We don't necessarily open their minds or change people, but they do respect that there are GLBT kids out there." Even in the classrooms of teachers who opposed the Safe Staff initiative, discriminatory references are no longer tolerated. And in several subject areas, GLBT issues are discussed more often. Gretzlock believes the climate in the high school has changed. She says, "There are a lot fewer blanket GLBT slurs. In large part, gone are the days of walking down the hall and hearing, 'That's so gay.'" When students do slip, they know immediately to apologize. But Gretzlock says the greatest testament to the change in atmosphere is when someone makes a comment and another student says, "*Gay* doesn't mean *stupid*."

ACTIVITY 16

Bully Role Play

Audience: Youth, peer helpers.

Focus: To give peer helpers an opportunity to practice the skills they need to support peer victims of bullying. This is an activity to use in conjunction with a more thorough training on bullying and peer helping.

You will need: Peer helpers, whiteboard.

Before the day: Choose two to three youth to role-play a brief bullying situation. Help them write a script and practice the role play. Give these youth an overview of the training that will occur that day so they can understand the skills the other peer helpers will be learning. Consider the questions in Step 1 when writing the script.

Set the stage: Discuss the ways bullying can hurt the victims, and explain that being a support for bullied youth is a critical role of peer helpers. This activity will help peer helpers practice acquiring the information needed to identify solutions to a problem. Although there are no clear-cut solutions to bullying episodes, knowing the questions to ask will help the peer helper and the victim work together to address the situation.

Step 1: Ask youth to talk about bullying situations they've witnessed or heard about in school. After a few stories have been shared, ask them to think about themselves as people who the victim might approach for help. Ask them to brainstorm solution-focused questions they might try to answer. Write these ideas on the whiteboard. Once youth have shared their ideas, also write out the following questions if they haven't already been addressed:

- How is the student being bullied?
- Why is the student being bullied?
- How is the student reacting? (Fighting back, ignoring them, crying.)
- Where are the teachers and administrators?
- Who else is in the hallway?
- How can the student stop the bullying? (Tell the teacher, counselor, friends; get friends to help.)
- What do we know about the student?

Step 2: Ask the role players to perform their skit. Then ask audience members to take turns asking the questions that will lead them to a solution for the bullied student.

Step 3: Brainstorm possible interventions the student could try to stop the bullying.

Reflection Questions:

• What other tools do you need in order to be successful in this process?

• If you use this skill, what possible changes could you expect to see in the school climate?

• Who else could be involved in learning about these interventions?

(Activity adapted with the permission of the National Association of Peer Programs from Andrew Beale and Kimberly Hall, "Solutions-Focused Role Play: Its Use in Training Peer Helpers," Peer Facilitator Quarterly, Winter/Spring 2005, 143–147.)

ACTIVITY 17

It's Policy

Audience: Youth.

Focus: To educate students about the school district's nondiscrimination policy so they know the expectations for their behavior in the building.

You will need: Copies of the policy for all staff facilitators, transparencies printed with main policy headings, overhead projector.

Before the day: Advisor/advisee rooms or homeroom classrooms are the best venue for this activity. Homeroom teachers must first receive in-service training on the nondiscrimination policy to clarify ambiguous statements and prepare to field student questions.

Set the stage: Explain to youth that the district takes discrimination seriously and wants to promote a respectful environment where all people are accepting of differences. Discussing the nondiscrimination policy adopted by the school district is one way to make sure that everyone understands the behavior that's expected at school.

Step 1: Discuss the word "discrimination." Ask youth what this word means to them and share stories about discriminatory situations they've witnessed or heard about.

Step 2: Introduce the district's nondiscrimination policy, and discuss what each part means. This type of policy is a legal commonality in any environment and details everyone's rights. Use the overhead projector to display transparencies.

Step 3: Answer questions youth have about the policy, and ask students the reflection questions that follow.

Reflection Questions:

• Why would a policy like this need to be written and mandated?

- Why are these groups addressed in the policy?
- How have your feelings about discrimination been affected as a result of this discussion?
- How could this discussion affect the school climate?

(Activity adapted with permission from New Richmond High School, New Richmond, Wisconsin.)

Working for Change

"When we ensure that basic human needs are met, we are creating a more secure world. When we work for social justice or to stop global warming, or to provide decent education, or to end racism, we are creating a more secure world. The time has come to shift our energy and our resources from military security to a long-term investment in true security."

—EXCERPT FROM *THE GLOBAL CALL TO ACTION*, LAUNCHED BY NOBEL PEACE LAUREATES AT PEACEJAM 2006, DENVER, COLORADO

In 2006, the PeaceJam Foundation—whose worldwide affiliates deliver community-based programs that seek to create young leaders committed to positive change based on the inspirational examples of Nobel Peace Prize winners—challenged youth from around the globe to join in working for societal change. Ten Nobel Laureates stated, "Over the next ten years, we hope to inspire over a billion acts of service and peace."

Inspirational and powerful change agents recognize the power youth have to find possible solutions to the world's ills, many of which relate to safety. The 10 Nobel Peace Prize Laureates who participated were the Dalai Lama, Archbishop Desmond Tutu, Rigoberta Menchú Tum, Costa Rican President Oscar Arias, Máiread Corrigan Maguire, Jody Williams, Shirin Ebadi, East Timor President José Ramos Horta, Adolfo Pérez Esquivel, and Betty Williams. The Global Call to Action issued by the laureates includes issues that might seem insurmountable even to adults. But by engaging young people in a worldwide campaign for positive change, who knows what might result? The Global Call to Action (www.globalcalltoaction.org) focuses on the following ten core problems:

- Unequal access to water and other natural resources
- Racism and hate
- The spread of global disease
- Extreme poverty
- Social justice and human rights for all
- Rights for women and children, and their role as leaders
- Environmental degradation
- Nuclear weapons and the international arms trade
- Disarming society's armed consciousness
- Focus on human security to create true security

Youthrive, the Upper Midwest affiliate of PeaceJam International, supports emerging young leaders and strengthens leadership and peace-building skills. It provides opportunities for diverse youth to engage in civic dialogue and action on issues of social justice, human rights, nonviolence, and antiracism.

Donna Gillen, executive director of youthrive, believes it isn't laws and metal detectors that will ensure society's security and safety in the long term, it's the ability of people to respect each other. Most of the time adults expect to be treated with respect by young people, but they don't always reciprocate. Gillen says:

> The way [youthrive does] business with young people is to treat them immediately with respect, no matter what. Our office is a safe space for kids to be who they are—to be real. It's an environment for trial and error, where it's okay to be who they are. When they foul up, they learn from their mistakes, and that's it. Put it to rest and go at it again. There's no judging.

Strong youth and adult relationships can make it easier for youth to step forward with information about potential danger. In an emotionally safe environment, a young person may tell an adult when she or he hears someone threaten violence.

If young people balk at seeking adult help because they don't think they're facing a serious threat, Gillen says an adult can walk the young person through important questions to help them assess the seriousness of a situation:

What's your responsibility? How can you help [other people] resolve the anger they feel? How can they get the help they need to work through it? Even if you think they're just joking, what's your responsibility since they're saying something?

Gillen praises the value of positive risk taking. She says parents should monitor their children's actions without limiting their sense of adventure. "You need to help them think through the consequences when they want to do something," she says. "The more they are allowed to make their own choices after thinking them through, the more they will be able to handle choices better on their own later." Gillen mentions a boy who decided to become a peacemaker after eating lunch with a Nobel Peace Prize Laureate: "It's like lightbulbs going on. They grow up with violence and incarceration . . . [but] if there is peace, there isn't a safety issue."

"There's a fine balance between support and being supported to take calculated risks," says John Ure, associate director of programs at Heartwood in Halifax, Nova Scotia. "We're not doing our young people any favors by making things *too* safe." He also says it can be healthy to provide youth with opportunities to step out of their comfort zones, make mistakes, and learn from them. "Safety is sometimes just being there to help them feel safe to do their thing." When he prepares youth for adventurous learning at Heartwood, Ure explains:

You'll be stepping out of your comfort zone, but we won't ask you to step out of your safety zone. You'll stretch yourself, push yourself, but you'll never be sent in a direction that would be dangerous—a physical or emotional risk.

Jim Cameron, team leader for PRIDE youth programs in Amarillo, Texas, views safety in a similar way. Most of PRIDE's clients are young people involved in the court system. All have had some level of drug or alcohol use, and many meet screening criteria on substance abuse and mental disorder inventories. PRIDE uses a ropes leadership course to focus on empowerment of their youth clients.

"For an adolescent to earn his way to thirty feet in the air is empowering—not to mention going down a zip line from fifty feet in the air," he says. Many of the tasks have to be done as a group, which encourages collaboration. Youth are also taught how to "spot" other participants. "This puts them in a situation in which another person's well-being is in their hands," Cameron says. "It requires the client to be responsible for another client's safety."

Youth Own the Climate

"Students voices are heard—they aren't afraid to express their opinions. They clearly have a role in decision making at their school site."

—LINDA SILVIUS, SCHOOL PARTNERSHIP DIRECTOR, PROJECT CORNERSTONE, SANTA CLARA COUNTY

Project Cornerstone in Santa Clara County, California, sponsors student workshops that teach youth how to nurture a caring climate in their schools. Facilitators challenge students to own the climate of their school by improving respect between students and reducing bullying and peer abuse. Each school team creates and implements an action plan designed to have a schoolwide impact.

Peer helpers can challenge stereotypes by taking a stand. Richmond High School in Indiana has experienced ongoing, disrespectful speech and actions toward its Hispanic students in town. Susan Routson, executive director of Peer Information Center for Teens (PICT) peer helpers, in Richmond, Indiana, says, "Hostile and homophobic attitudes of a significant number of students make RHS halls an unfriendly place for some students." To address the prejudice, PICT peer helpers participate in "Partners Against Hate" training and coordinate nondiscrimination programs such as "Mix It Up at Lunch" and "No Name-Calling Week" for over 1,600 Richmond High School students.

Even youth who don't participate in organized efforts can positively influence school climate. The "Bully-Proofing Your School" program involves mobilizing the caring majority of students. The goal is to shift power away from the bullies to the "silent majority" bystanders who typically witness bullying but do nothing to intervene. As part of a comprehensive approach, the program teaches this silent majority to become the caring majority. Empowering and supporting youth bystanders to stand up against bullies can curb aggressive behavior.[11]

Empowered youth help facilitate change, and if provided with the right tools, they can learn to take control in an unsafe situation. The city of Georgetown, Texas, implemented a Safe Place campaign for young people. A logo designed by middle school youth is displayed on all the utility trucks in the city. City workers receive training on the importance of the Developmental Assets and what to do if a child needing assistance approaches them. Electric company employees go into classrooms and teach children to look for the Safe Place logo. If kids see a utility truck with this sign, they know it's a safe place to ask for help.

Get on the Bus!

"Central to school safety are the supportive bonds with adults who help create school climates free of bullying."

—MICHAEL DORN, SCHOOL SAFETY EXPERT AND AUTHOR OF
WEAKFISH: BULLYING THROUGH THE EYES OF A CHILD

Unfortunately, the school bus is often a dangerous place for kids. Although a video camera can be an effective deterrent to bad behavior, as well as an investigative tool after the fact, it's the bus driver who ultimately sets the tone for riders' behavior. While bus drivers train to safely maneuver their vehicles and effectively handle emergency situations, many are ill-equipped to manage their passengers.

Bus drivers at Pointers Run Elementary School receive a new mug each year, and inside the mug is a card laminated with strategies they can use to create a safe bus environment. Drivers discuss these "rules of the road" with their passengers at the beginning of each school year. Youth are expected to participate in creating that safe environment—to help the driver do her or his job and make the ride more enjoyable for everyone. Bus drivers also learn ways to connect with the young passengers, greeting them and saying good-bye, listening to their conversations, and interacting with them in a thoughtful way.

ESTABLISHING RULES OF THE ROAD

- What behavior do we need on the bus?
- How can we reward the good stuff?
- How can we appreciate those who make the ride better?
- What are some things each of us can do to make a better ride each day?
- What should the driver do when someone's behavior gets out of line?
- Should the driver be the only one who enforces the rules? Who else can do it?

(Adapted with permission from Pass it On at School!, *Search Institute, 2003.)*

Building a Safe Environment

"First, listen; be willing to put your thoughts and opinions aside; and be open to new and creative ways of doing things. Be committed to not just giving youth a voice in theory, but truly giving them a voice."

—LESLIE JANCA, COORDINATOR FOR THE GEORGETOWN PROJECT

The design and structure of schools can help make them warm and caring places in which children can succeed. Effective design of the physical environment can also help minimize safety issues. Administrators need to know the threat level of their school.

Perhaps the best way to empower youth with regard to their safety is to recognize them as stakeholders in their own safety. In the aftermath of school violence elsewhere, school personnel often scramble to ensure their safety measures will function properly in the case of a tragic event. But how often do school leaders ask for input from youth? Julia Hampton, Windham County Youth Initiative Coordinator, says schools should call on youth to help determine the protocol for safety drills.

The high school in her town sponsored a safety retreat. Hampton says, "The kids problem-solved to work out the kinks. They also brainstormed about the lockdown drill—how could it be made better? Like, what if they get stuck in the bathroom?" Also, the school installed a new identification system for youth, and it was youth who suggested that visitors swipe a card as they entered. It made an instant ID check for criminal background.

Including youth in the process of designing safe and effective security procedures for their schools and places where they gather has the added benefit of addressing community-wide safety issues as well. The Georgetown Project led a community task force on diversity issues, prompted by a racially charged incident at the local high school. For six months, the Georgetown Youth Action Council participated in leadership and diversity training and meetings to discuss tolerance, respect, and ways to bring youth together to talk about differences. Finally, the council hosted a youth summit and received a loud, clear message from youth: "We want a safe place to go where we're not pressured to do things we know we shouldn't."

The group discussed their findings with the Georgetown city council, and the city put together a multimillion-dollar bond package to finance the expansion of the existing recreation center, including space for a new teen center. Youth wrote grants for the project and participated in the planning process to determine what the center would look like inside and the kinds of programs that would be offered so that a variety of young people would feel comfortable and included.

Youth suggested a diverse set of activities and an inclusive environment for the teen center: one that featured a computer room, a tutoring area, a space to perform music, recite poetry, and showcase their artistic talents, a coffeehouse, and a place where kids could reach out to the community. They even suggested it be open to senior citizens by day and to teens at night. There could be an indoor pool for the youth swim team and senior aerobics classes.

Leslie Janca, coordinator for the Georgetown Project, says, "The kids were the ones who took it beyond ethnic diversity. They said, 'That's a given—if you cover a diverse set of interests, you'll probably get a diverse set of kids too.'" The Georgetown Teen Center will open in 2009.

Youth as Resources in Safety

*"Adults cannot discount the influence they
can have in young people's lives."*

—REBECCA JARVIS, CNBC TELEVISION BUSINESS CORRESPONDENT

In January 2007, 15-year-old Mitchell Hults watched his friend, Ben, disappear down the hill in front of him. Shortly after, he noticed a white pickup truck speeding down the road. When Ben's parents called Mitchell later to ask if he'd seen Ben, he said he hadn't for some time and then relayed the story of the white pickup. Mitchell gave the police a full description of the vehicle, recalling even the smallest details— how many windows it had, its missing hubcaps, and the kind of handle on the tailgate. After four days of investigation, police found both Ben *and* another boy who had been kidnapped four years earlier by the same man. Police honored Mitchell for his keen awareness and encouraged him to find work in law enforcement when he grows older.

In the same month, a woman and her four children were kidnapped in Elkhart, Indiana. They were rescued after an 18-year-old pizza deliveryman, Derek Powers, recognized the man who had abducted them from police reports. These young people were key witnesses to crimes that could have ended tragically had adults not considered the importance of their testimony. They were clearly public safety resources. Young people have the ability to influence our world more significantly than we may ever know.

ACTIVITY 18

Safe Design

Audience: Youth and adults.

Focus: To tap into youth expertise and experience to design a building that serves youth.

You will need: Chart paper, whiteboard, markers, tables to accommodate small groups.

Before the day: Ideally, participants will have had an opportunity to tour newer buildings or research safe building designs. Otherwise, it may be helpful to create a list of safety considerations prior to the design day.

Set the stage: Because the group is constructing a new building (school, place of worship, community center), members have a unique opportunity to include modern amenities and features that address safety concerns. The purpose of this planning day is to generate ideas from youth and adults to make sure the design team has as much information as possible as they plan the building. Youth have a unique perspective that most adults do not have, so their input is critical.

Step 1: As a large group, brainstorm on a whiteboard the major sections of the building to be constructed.

Step 2: In small groups, participants need to write the title of each major building area at the top of separate sheets of paper. Teams will brainstorm a list of questions and safety issues for each area on the left side of the paper, and possible solutions on the right side. Encourage participants to be detailed in their brainstorming about potential safety concerns and to be creative in their solutions. At this stage in the process, no criticism is allowed. All ideas should be included on the list, and adults and youth are expected to contribute ideas to each area. Also consider how lockdowns and fire drills will be addressed.

Step 3: Finally, groups can draw the outline of their proposed building, writing problems and solutions where they occur. All groups share their maps, and the building designer takes the ideas to the next stage of the process.

Reflection Questions:

- What safety concerns and solutions had you not considered before the brainstorming?
- How could this process ultimately influence the future building project?
- In what other community projects could a youth perspective be useful?

ACTIVITY 19

Switch!

Audience: Youth.

Focus: To encourage youth to cross social boundaries and help them discover ways in which they're the same.

You will need: Youth facilitators, poster board for signs.

Before the day: Choose topics with the help of youth facilitators. Look for topics that are fun and that challenge youth to move beyond their established friend groups. Sample categories could include zodiac sign, favorite color, eye color, family heritage, number of siblings, or favorite extracurricular activity. Train youth leaders to manage small-group conversations during each topic change in order to encourage students to see each other as more alike than they previously thought. Have youth leaders practice asking basic questions, such as, "Why did you choose this group as your answer? Tell us about it." Have facilitators help you make signs so that students will have a visual aid to figure out where they're going when they make the "Switch!"

Set the stage: Teachers and youth facilitators discuss with students why it's important to respect differences while also recognizing how much alike all people are. Ask discussion questions, such as "In what ways are the students in this school different? In what ways are they alike? Where do cultural differences cause conflict in the world? What actions could help create peace?"

Step 1: Tell students they are to look for answers to the questions you'll be asking by locating them on a sign held by one of the group leaders. Ask the first question (preferably one that's simple to answer and hard to fake). Youth group leaders help their groups to converse, encouraging people to share their names and explain how they fit within the category represented by that group. Conversation can be relaxed discussion about the ways in which people are similar. After a couple of minutes, blow a whistle to end the conversation, ask the next question, and say "Switch!"

Step 2: Continue the process as long as you like. Each conversation can last as long as most youth are engaged in the activity.

Step 3: After the final question, ask group reflection questions to process what people have learned about each other.

Reflection Questions:

- What new information did you learn about a classmate that you didn't already know?
- What surprised you?
- Did you find another classmate who answered questions in much the same way as you did?
- How could this exercise positively affect our school climate and the way we see each other at school?

(Activity adapted with permission from New Richmond High School, New Richmond, Wisconsin.)

Expanding from "Me" to "We"

- Engage other adults and youth in discussions about safety. What concerns do they have?

- Do youth understand the concerns we have as adults?

- Join or initiate a neighborhood watch organization.

- Attend forums like PeaceJam to learn more about global security and empower youth to plan and carry out a significant action.

- Reach out to parents in the neighborhood, as friends and "partner parents."

- Welcome the children of these parents into your home to engage in healthy, safe, fun activities.

- Write or talk to civic leaders and offer input on ways to create safer environments for kids.

Did You Know?

Fifteen-year-old Dallas Jessup, Prudential Spirit of Community Awards honoree from Vancouver, Washington, cowrote and starred in the 45-minute film *Just Yell Fire* to teach girls how to fight off attackers. Dallas holds a black belt in tae kwon do, but realized not every girl knows how to defend herself. After watching footage of an abduction on TV news, Dallas asked her martial arts coach to develop some simple self-defense strategies that a 100-pound girl could use to get away from a 250-pound attacker. Her project snowballed into a major production with a professional crew and a 100-member cast, including actors from the television show *Lost*. More than 14,000 people downloaded the video during the first 20 days it appeared on the Web site justyellfire.com.

Epilogue

*"There are sprinters and there are marathon
runners. In building assets, we need both—
for the short-term burst of speed and power, as
well as the long-term energy and endurance."*

—MARILYN PEPLAU, TRAINER, SEARCH INSTITUTE VISION TRAINING ASSOCIATES

Marilyn Peplau, my longtime mentor in the "asset approach," once
shared with me her philosophy about sprinters and marathon runners.
Sprinters tackle a project, jump on a bandwagon, offer an opportunity, or fund an initiative. They believe in positive youth development
research and the words of asset champions who tell them it's the right
thing to do for kids. They're willing to take a chance on an activity
because someone they respect thinks it's a great idea.

What would we do without the store owners who stuff grocery
bags with local asset-based carnival flyers? The retired teacher who
volunteers to read books in kindergarten classrooms? The local banker
who serves on the United Way board and carefully considers and funds
excellent proposals for and by youth? The contractor who joins in a
youth service project to provide leadership and assistance to a group
of young people? The city manager who provides the administrative
logistics to organize a youth summit? The principal who invites students to share opinions regarding safety in their school?

After completing their project, service initiative, or meeting, these
Developmental Asset sprinters may return to their daily responsibilities in environments that don't lend themselves to much youth
involvement. They might proceed in their regular routines, with little
participation in the asset initiative brewing in their community. They
may give themselves fully to the cause just once per month or even
once per year, and then leave the work to others, until it's again their
turn to serve.

Sprinters make their mark, and fill a need that others can't. And
their involvement makes them better versed in the importance of
building assets. Sprinters can become asset ambassadors, providing a

sometimes subtle but vital link to an adult population that would otherwise remain untapped.

And then there are marathon runners.

I interviewed many marathon runners in the course of writing this book. They're the people whose life philosophy completely embraces the asset-building approach. Asking for youth input is as common a practice as brushing one's teeth. Marathon runners "own" a philosophy that naturally includes a discussion about young people in most decisions. When community projects are to be completed, their first questions address the ways in which youth can be consulted, included, and served. And the power of their influence lies not only in the ways they spread the good news about youth but also in how they authentically live the philosophy, expecting and encouraging the best from youth and adults. Marathon runners are models for the rest of us.

If you've read this book, you most likely fit into one of these roles, or perhaps can see situations in which you serve in each role. How are you a sprinter? How are you a marathon runner? Either way, you're serving the needs of young people, and the inherent differences between these two roles allow so many more young people to be reached. Every step you take toward building assets in youth is a step in the right direction.

At the beginning of this book, I introduced the three-legged seat of empowerment, an image that suggests three keys to adopting a philosophy of empowering young people: *See youth, teach youth,* and *believe in youth.* This is the basic foundation for strengthening the Empowerment assets in our youth—recognizing young people as valuable, full citizens within our communities and paving the way for them to use their special talents in ways that improve society as a whole.

When you intentionally build these "legs" every day or on a regular basis, you make a difference in the lives of young people; in the lives of youth and adults who are touched by those young people; in the way your community functions; and in the way society views youth. If you look closely, you're also making a difference in yourself—*thank you.*

Search Institute's Framework of 40 Developmental Assets® for Adolescents (ages 12 to 18)

*Search Institute® has identified the following building blocks of healthy develop-
ment—known as Developmental Assets—that help young people grow up healthy,
caring, and responsible.*

EXTERNAL ASSETS

Support

1. **Family Support**—Family life provides high levels of love and support.
2. **Positive Family Communication**—Young person and her or his parent(s)
   communicate positively, and young person is willing to seek advice and counsel
   from parent(s).
3. **Other Adult Relationships**—Young person receives support from three or more
   nonparent adults.
4. **Caring Neighborhood**—Young person experiences caring neighbors.
5. **Caring School Climate**—School provides a caring, encouraging environment.
6. **Parent Involvement in Schooling**—Parent(s) are actively involved in helping
   young person succeed in school.

Empowerment

7. **Community Values Youth**—Young person perceives that adults in the
   community value youth.
8. **Youth as Resources**—Young people are given useful roles in the community.
9. **Service to Others**—Young person serves in the community one hour or more
   per week.
10. **Safety**—Young person feels safe at home, at school, and in the neighborhood.

Boundaries & Expectations

11. **Family Boundaries**—Family has clear rules and consequences and monitors the
    young person's whereabouts.

12. **School Boundaries**—School provides clear rules and consequences.

13. **Neighborhood Boundaries**—Neighbors take responsibility for monitoring young people's behavior.

14. **Adult Role Models**—Parent(s) and other adults model positive, responsible behavior.

15. **Positive Peer Influence**—Young person's best friends model responsible behavior.

16. **High Expectations**—Both parent(s) and teachers encourage the young person to do well.

Constructive Use of Time

17. **Creative Activities**—Young person spends three or more hours per week in lessons or practice in music, theater, or other arts.

18. **Youth Programs**—Young person spends three or more hours per week in sports, clubs, or organizations at school and/or in the community.

19. **Religious Community**—Young person spends one or more hours per week in activities in a religious institution.

20. **Time at Home**—Young person is out with friends "with nothing special to do" two or fewer nights per week.

INTERNAL ASSETS

Commitment to Learning

21. **Achievement Motivation**—Young person is motivated to do well in school.

22. **School Engagement**—Young person is actively engaged in learning.

23. **Homework**—Young person reports doing at least one hour of homework every school day.

24. **Bonding to School**—Young person cares about her or his school.

25. **Reading for Pleasure**—Young person reads for pleasure three or more hours per week.

Positive Values

26. **Caring**—Young person places high value on helping other people.

27. **Equality and Social Justice**—Young person places high value on promoting equality and reducing hunger and poverty.

28. **Integrity**—Young person acts on convictions and stands up for her or his beliefs.

29. **Honesty**—Young person "tells the truth even when it is not easy."

30. **Responsibility**—Young person accepts and takes personal responsibility.

31. **Restraint**—Young person believes it is important not to be sexually active or to use alcohol or other drugs.

Social Competencies

32. **Planning and Decision Making**—Young person knows how to plan ahead and make choices.

33. **Interpersonal Competence**—Young person has empathy, sensitivity, and friendship skills.

34. **Cultural Competence**—Young person has knowledge of and comfort with people of different cultural/racial/ethnic backgrounds.

35. **Resistance Skills**—Young person can resist negative peer pressure and dangerous situations.

36. **Peaceful Conflict Resolution**—Young person seeks to resolve conflict nonviolently.

Positive Identity

37. **Personal Power**—Young person feels he or she has control over "things that happen to me."

38. **Self-Esteem**—Young person reports having a high self-esteem.

39. **Sense of Purpose**—Young person reports that "my life has a purpose."

40. **Positive View of Personal Future**—Young person is optimistic about her or his personal future.

This list may be reproduced for educational, noncommercial uses only. Copyright ©1997, 2006 by Search Institute. Reprinted with permission from *Empowering Youth: How to Encourage Young Leaders to Do Great Things*, by Kelly Curtis, M.S. Copyright © 2008 by Search Institute, Minneapolis, Minnesota, 800-888-7828, www.search-institute.org. All rights reserved.

Notes

Introduction

1. Search Institute, *Developmental Assets: A Profile of Your Youth—Search Institute 2003 Weighted Aggregate Dataset* (Minneapolis: Search Institute, 2005).

Chapter 1

1. Shepherd Zeldin, *Adult Beliefs about Youth as Contributors to Community*, Unpublished data (Madison: University of Wisconsin, 2000). Referenced in S. Zeldin, A.K. McDaniel, D. Topitzes, and M. Calvert, *Youth in Decision Making: A Study on the Impact of Youth on Adults and Organizations* (Chevy Chase, MD: National 4-H Council, 2000).

Chapter 2

1. Elaine Doremus Slayton, *Empowering Teens: A Guide to Developing a Community-Based Youth Organization* (Chicago: CROYA, 2000), 20–23. Adapted with permission of the author.

2. Slayton, *Empowering Teens*. Adapted with permission of the author.

3. Cathann A. Kress, "Youth Leadership and Youth Development: Connections and Questions," *New Directions for Youth Development* 109 (2006): 45–56, © 2006 by John Wiley & Sons, Inc. All rights reserved. Reprinted with permission.

4. Carole MacNeil, "Bridging Generations: Applying 'Adult' Leadership Theories to Youth Leadership Development," *New Directions for Youth Development* 109 (2006): 27–43, © 2006 by John Wiley & Sons, Inc. All rights reserved. Reprinted with permission.

5. The Freedom Writers, with Erin Gruwell, *The Freedom Writers Diary: How a Teacher and 150 Teens Used Writing to Change Themselves and the World Around Them* (New York: Doubleday, 1999), 81.

6. Jill Denner, Beth Meyer, and Steve Bean, "Young Women's Leadership Alliance: Youth-Adult Partnerships in an All-Female After-School Program," *Journal of Community Psychology* 33:1 (2005): 87–100. © 2005 by John Wiley & Sons, Inc. All rights reserved. Reprinted with permission.

7. Karen Young, Jenny Sazama, and Kathryn Jones, *14 Points: Successfully Involving Youth in Decision Making* (Somerville, MA: Youth on Board, 1999).

8. Carole MacNeil and Jennifer McClean, "Moving from 'Youth Leadership Development' to 'Youth in Governance': Learning Leadership by Doing Leadership,"

New Directions for Youth Development 109 (2006): 99–106, © 2006 by John Wiley & Sons, Inc. All rights reserved. Reprinted with permission.

Chapter 3

1. Peter C. Scales and Eugene C. Roehlkepartain, "Service to Others: A 'Gateway Asset' for School Success and Healthy Development," in *Growing to Greatness 2004: The State of Service-Learning in the United States* (St. Paul, MN: National Youth Leadership Council, 2004).

2. Christopher Toppe, Silvia Golombek, et al. *Engaging Youth in Lifelong Service* (Washington, DC: Independent Sector, 2002); Linda J. Sax, Alexander W. Astin, W.S. Korn, and K.M. Mahoney, *The American Freshman: National Norms for Fall 1999* (Los Angeles: UCLA, Higher Education Research Institute, 2000); Rebecca Skinner and Chris Chapman, *Service Learning and Community Service in K–12 Public Schools* (Washington, DC: U.S. Department of Education National Center for Education Statistics, 1999); Search Institute, *Developmental Assets: A Profile of Your Youth.*

3. Verna Cornelia Simmons and Pam Toole, "Service-Learning Diversity/Equity Project Research Report Executive Summary," *Generator,* St. Paul: National Youth Leadership Council, Summer 2003.

4. Scales and Roehlkepartain, "Service to Others."

5. David R. Black, Ph.D., Elizabeth Foster-Harrison, Ed.D., Judy Tindall, Ph.D., JoLynn Johnson, Barbara Varenhorst, Ph.D., Sara Moscato, M.S., "Selected Peer Resource Literature," *Peer Facilitator Quarterly* 17:1 (2003): 14–21.

6. Judith A. Tindall, Leonard Taylor, and Lois Williams, "In the Field: St. Louis Job Corps—Trainee Led Mentor Program," *Peer Facilitator Quarterly* 19:1 (2005): 86–88.

7. Silvia Blitzer Golombek, "National Youth Service Day: A Youth Development Strategy," *Journal of Youth Development* 1:1 (2006), © 2006 by *Journal of Youth Development.* Reprinted with permission.

Chapter 4

1. Search Institute, *Developmental Assets: A Profile of Your Youth.*

2. Andrea Billups, "School Violence," *Washington Times* 8:36 (2001): 1, 23.

3. Curtis N. Rhodes, Jr., Haytham A. Mihyar, and Ghada Abu El-Rous, "Social Learning and Community Participation with Children at Risk in Two Marginalized Urban Neighborhoods in Amman, Jordan," in *Youth in Cities: A Cross-National Perspective,* edited by Marta Tienda and William Julius Wilson (Cambridge, UK: Cambridge University Press, 2002), 191–214.

4. David S. Derezotes, Deb Ashton, and Tracie L. Hoffman, "The Voices Project," *Child and Adolescent Social Work Journal* 21:3 (2004): 237–264.

5. Dan Olweus, *Bullying at School: What We Know and What We Can Do*, (Oxford: Blackwell Publishers, 1993), cited in Dufresne and Dorn, "Keeping Students and Schools Safe," *Reclaiming Children and Youth* 14:2 (2005): 93–96.

6. Jerilyn Dufresne, with Michael Dorn, "Keeping Students and Schools Safe," *Reclaiming Children and Youth* 14:2 (2005): 93–96.

7. Erik K. Laursen. "Rather than Fixing Kids—Build Positive Peer Cultures," *Reclaiming Children and Youth: The Journal of Strength-Based Interventions* 14:3 (2005): 137–142.

8. "Hollywood, Government and Youth Mobilize to Counter Recent Teen Crashes," *The Peer Facilitator Quarterly* (Winter/Spring 2005).

9. Search Institute, *Developmental Assets: A Profile of Your Youth*.

10. Timothy C. Smith, *Crashproof Your Kids: Make Your Teen a Safer, Smarter Driver* (New York: Simon & Schuster, 2006).

11. Marla Bonds and Sally Stoker, *Bully-Proofing Your School: A Comprehensive Approach for Middle Schools* (Longmont, CO: Sopris West, 2000).

Bibliography

Benson, Peter L., Judy Galbraith, and Pamela Espeland. *What Kids Need to Succeed: Proven, Practical Ways to Raise Good Kids,* Minneapolis: Free Spirit Publishing, 1998, 56.

Billups, Andrea. "School Violence," *Washington Times,* 8:36 (2001), 1, 23.

Black, David R., Ph.D., Elizabeth Foster-Harrison, Ed.D., Judy Tindall, Ph.D., JoLynn Johnson, Barbara Varenhorst, Ph.D., and Sara Moscato, M.S. "Selected Peer Resource Literature," *Peer Facilitator Quarterly,* 17:1 (2003), 14–21.

Bonds, Marla, and Sally Stoker. *Bully-Proofing Your School: A Comprehensive Approach for Middle Schools,* Longmont, CO: Sopris West, 2000.

Carlson, Cindy. "The Hampton Experience as a New Model for Youth Civic Engagement," *Journal of Community Practice,* 14:1/2 (2006), 89–106.

Denner, Jill, Beth Meyer, and Steve Bean. "Young Women's Leadership Alliance: Youth-Adult Partnerships in an All-Female After-School Program," *Journal of Community Psychology,* 33:1 (2005), 87–100.

Derezotes, David S., Deb Ashton, and Tracie L. Hoffman. "The Voices Project," *Child and Adolescent Social Work Journal,* 21:3 (2004), 237–264.

Dufresne, Jerilyn, with Michael Dorn. "Keeping Students and Schools Safe," *Reclaiming Children and Youth: The Journal of Strength-Based Interventions,* 14:2 (2005), 93–96.

Fisher, Deborah. *Working Shoulder to Shoulder: Stories and Strategies of Youth-Adult Partnerships That Succeed,* Minneapolis: Search Institute, 2004.

The Freedom Writers, with Erin Gruwell. *The Freedom Writers Diary: How a Teacher and 150 Teens Used Writing to Change Themselves and the World Around Them,* New York: Doubleday, 1999, 81.

Golombek, Silvia Blitzer. "Children as Citizens," *Journal of Community Practice,* 14:1/2 (2006), 11–30.

Golombek, Silvia Blitzer. "National Youth Service Day: A Youth Development Strategy," *Journal of Youth Development,* 1:1 (2006).

Grothe, Rebecca. *More Building Assets Together,* Minneapolis: Search Institute, 2002.

Hart, Roger A. "Children's Participation: from Tokenism to Citizenship," *Innocenti Essays No. 4*, Florence, Italy: UNICEF International Child Development Centre, 1992.

"Hollywood, Government and Youth Mobilize to Counter Recent Teen Crashes," press release, National Highway Transportation Safety Administration, October 15, 2004.

Kress, Cathann A. "Youth Leadership and Youth Development: Connections and Questions," *New Directions for Youth Development*, 109 (2006), 45–56.

Laursen, Erik K. "Rather than Fixing Kids—Build Positive Peer Cultures," *Reclaiming Children and Youth: The Journal of Strength-Based Interventions*, 14:3 (2005): 137–142.

Lofquist, William A. "The Spectrum of Adult Attitudes Toward Young People," *The Technology of Prevention Workbook*, Tuscon: Associates for Youth Development, 1989, 47–50.

MacNeil, Carole A. "Bridging Generations: Applying 'Adult' Leadership Theories to Youth Leadership Development," *New Directions for Youth Development*, 109 (2006), 27–43.

MacNeil, Carole A., with Jennifer McClean. "Moving from 'Youth Leadership Development' to 'Youth in Governance': Learning Leadership by Doing Leadership," *New Directions for Youth Development*, 109 (2006), 99–106.

Olweus, Dan. *Bullying at School: What We Know and What We Can Do*, Oxford: Blackwell Publishers, 1993, cited in Dufresne and Dorn, "Keeping Students and Schools Safe," *Reclaiming Children and Youth*, 14:2 (2005), 93–96.

"Report: Best Urban Practices Fair," *Universal Forum of Cultures*, Forum Barcelona 2004, September 2004.

Rhodes, Curtis N., Jr., Haytham A. Mihyar, and Ghada Abu El-Rous. "Social Learning and Community Participation with Children at Risk in Two Marginalized Urban Neighborhoods in Amman, Jordan," in *Youth in Cities: A Cross-National Perspective*. Edited by Marta Tienda and William Julius Wilson. Cambridge, UK: Cambridge University Press, 2002, 191–214.

Roehlkepartain, Jolene, ed. *Pass It On!*, Minneapolis: Search Institute, 2006.

Sax, Linda J., Alexander W. Astin, W.S. Korn, and K.M. Mahoney. *The American Freshman: National Norms for Fall 1999*, Los Angeles: UCLA, Higher Education Research Institute, 2000.

Scales, Peter C., and Eugene C. Roehlkepartain. "Service to Others: A 'Gateway Asset' for School Success and Healthy Development," in *Growing to Greatness 2004: The State of Service-Learning in the United States*, St. Paul, MN: National Youth Leadership Council, 2004.

Search Institute. *Developmental Assets: A Profile of Your Youth—Search Institute 2003 Weighted Aggregate Dataset*, Minneapolis: Search Institute, 2005.

Search Institute. *The Power of Youth and Adult Partnerships and Change Pathways for Youth Work*, Minneapolis: Search Institute, 2005.

Simmons, Verna C., and Pam Toole. "Service-Learning Diversity/Equity Project Research Report Executive Summary," *Generator*, St. Paul: National Youth Leadership Council, Summer 2003.

Skinner, Rebecca, and Chris Chapman. *Service Learning and Community Service in K–12 Public Schools*, Washington, DC: U.S. Department of Education National Center for Education Statistics, 1999.

Slayton, Elaine Doremus. *Empowering Teens: A Guide to Developing a Community-Based Youth Organization*, Chicago: CROYA, 2000, 20–23.

Smith, Timothy C. *Crashproof Your Kids: Make Your Teen a Safer, Smarter Driver*, New York: Simon & Schuster, 2006.

Tindall, Judith A., Leonard Taylor, and Lois Williams. "In the Field: St. Louis Job Corps—Trainee Led Mentor Program," *The Peer Facilitator Quarterly*, 19:1 (2005), 86–88.

Toppe, Christopher, Silvia Golombek, et al. *Engaging Youth in Lifelong Service*, Washington, DC: Independent Sector, 2002.

Young, Karen, Jenny Sazama, and Kathryn Jones. *14 Points: Successfully Involving Youth in Decision Making*, Somerville, MA: Youth on Board, 1999.

Zeldin, Shepherd. *Adult Beliefs about Youth as Contributors to Community* (unpublished data), Madison, WI: University of Wisconsin, 2000. Referenced in S. Zeldin, A. K. McDaniel, D. Topitzes, and M. Calvert. *Youth in Decision Making: A Study on the Impact of Youth on Adults and Organizations*, Chevy Chase, MD: National 4-H Council (www.AtTheTable.org), 2000.

Zeldin, Shepherd. "Sense of Community and Positive Adult Beliefs toward Adolescents and Youth Policy in Urban Neighborhoods and Small Cities," *Journal of Youth and Adolescence: A Multidisciplinary Research Publication*, 31:5 (2002), 331–342.

Index

About the Author

Kelly Curtis is a school counselor, writer, speaker, and believer in the power of the Developmental Asset approach. In 2001, she founded Empowering Youth, Inc., which publishes positive youth development curricula, including the *SPARK Peer Tutoring Handbook and Training Manual,* and *Hidden Treasure of Assets* and *Career Expedition* board games. Kelly writes regularly about her experiences with children, parenthood, and family travel on her Web log, Pass the Torch, and she's been published in numerous anthologies and magazines across the United States. She lives in northwestern Wisconsin with her husband and two children. To learn more about Kelly, please visit her Web sites at kellycurtis.com and empowering-youth.com.

Reviewer Acknowledgments

Search Institute extends sincere thanks to the following individuals who reviewed an early draft of the manuscript and added their professional insights: Donna Bookout, Karrie Craig, Patti A. Davis, Alison Dotson, Betsy Gabler, Debbie Grillo, Julie Hudash, Kainette Jones, Wendi Keene, Erika Klein, Melissa Payk, Anne R. Ricciuti, Art Sesma, Dan Urra, Sandy Vogt.